Praise for *this* CHEESE *is nuts!*

"Julie Piatt has created a masterful and stylish book about one of my favorite things to eat, plant-based cheeses. *This Cheese Is Nuts!* includes all of the elements a great book on this subject should, including original, contemporary recipes; detailed instruction related to equipment and technique; and just the right amount of WHY, the reason this way of eating and living is so relevant today, and to the future of our society, our animals, and our planet. This is by far the most comprehensive, well-produced book I have seen on the subject."

—Matthew Kenney, chef

"Cheese was the final frontier when I decided to remove animal products from my diet, but the idea of re-creating those rich and intense flavors has always seemed daunting. Julie has masterfully opened up a whole new world in *This Cheese Is Nuts!* With crystal-clear instructions, a knack for streamlining the process, and warm encouragement that radiates from the page, you'll be enjoying her delicious dairy-free cheeses in no time. The best part? Your body will thank you for it."

—Laura Wright, author of *The First Mess Cookbook*

"We've all heard it before, 'I can't give up cheese!' *This Cheese Is Nuts!* turns obstacles into opportunities with mouthwatering recipes that are as easy as they are delicious, allowing the reader to lean into a plant-based diet without sacrificing taste or experience! A must-read and -do for anyone who loves cheese!"

—Marco Borges, author of *The 22-Day Revolution*

"Being a certified cheese addict while also being 100 percent vegan used to be a problem—but no more! Julie's recipes for plant-based cheese are divine and decadent, and have allowed me to return to my old obsession, albeit an upgraded and healthier one! You're gonna LOVE."

—Kathy Freston, *New York Times*–bestselling author *The Lean*, *Veganist*, and *Quantum Wellness*

"Julie Piatt is my culinary and lifestyle role model. Her knowledge and passion are top shelf. *This Cheese Is Nuts!* is packed with useful and inspiring information and easy-to-make mouthwatering cheeses, and makes a ridiculously healthy and vibrant lifestyle approachable and fun."

—Tara Stiles, founder of Strala

this CHEESE *is nuts!*

DELICIOUS VEGAN CHEESE AT HOME

JULIE PIATT

AVERY
AN IMPRINT OF PENGUIN RANDOM HOUSE
NEW YORK

AVERY

an imprint of Penguin Random House LLC
375 Hudson Street
New York, New York 10014

Most Avery books are available at special quantity discounts for
bulk purchase for sales promotions, premiums, fund-raising, and
educational needs. Special books or book excerpts also can be
created to fit specific needs. For details, write SpecialMarkets@
penguinrandomhouse.com.

Library of Congress Cataloging-in-Publication Data

Names: Piatt, Julie, author.
Title: This cheese is nuts! : delicious vegan cheese at home / Julie Piatt.
Description: New York, New York : Avery, an imprint of
  Penguin Random House, [2017] | Includes bibliographical
  references and index.
Identifiers: LCCN 2017012316| ISBN 9780735213791 (pbk.) |
  ISBN 9780735213807 (ebook)
Subjects: LCSH: Vegan cooking. | Cheese--Varieties. |
  Dairy substitutes. | LCGFT: Cookbooks.
Classification: LCC TX837 .P526 2017 | DDC 641.5/636--dc23
  LC record available at https://lccn.loc.gov/2017012316
  p.   cm.

Printed in the United States of America
10 9 8 7 6 5 4 3 2 1

Book design by Ashley Tucker

Neither the publisher nor the author is engaged in rendering
professional advice or services to the individual reader. The ideas,
procedures, and suggestions contained in this book are not intended
as a substitute for consulting with your physician. All matters
regarding your health require medical supervision. Neither the
author nor the publisher shall be liable or responsible for any loss
or damage allegedly arising from any information or suggestion in
this book.

The recipes contained in this book have been created for the
ingredients and techniques indicated. The publisher is not
responsible for your specific health or allergy needs that may
require supervision. Nor is the publisher responsible for any adverse
reactions you may have to the recipes contained in the book,
whether you follow them as written or modify them to suit your
personal dietary needs or tastes.

FOR GAIA AND
ALL HER CHILDREN

CONTENTS

INTRODUCTION

Welcome to the wonderful world of creamy and delicious plant-based cheese!

I am literally over the *Swiss cheese* moon to offer you this paradigm-breaking recipe collection of irresistible plant-based cheeses. In *The Plantpower Way: Whole Food Plant-Based Recipes and Guidance for the Whole Family* that I wrote with my husband, vegan endurance athlete and wellness podcast host, Rich Roll, I included some great basic, easy-to-prepare vegan cheese recipes that we adore. But since then, I've been dreaming of creating a cookbook that takes vegan cheese to the next level. For me, vegan cheese is the next frontier in my goal to help people eat delicious food while also living a healthy and conscious life. And I know that the biggest question most people have when they consider adopting a plant-based lifestyle is: How can I live without cheese and dairy? I'm thrilled to present this book as the best answer to that question. Problem solved! In fact, it's quite the opposite. I've put my heart and soul into creating these wildly delicious and creative recipes. You'll be amazed at how simple and delicious homemade vegan cheese can be!

We all love the rich flavor and creamy texture of cheese. For me, cheese is linked with my memories of living in Paris in my college years. My love for French cheese is true, but I had to find a way to create it in an entirely new way, one that is in alignment with compassion and sustainable living. And so during my process of experimenting with plant-based cheese, I've always been looking to re-create that taste and sense of indulgence. What I didn't expect is that it is possible to make plant-based cheeses that not only rival the best cheeses of France but are actually even *better*. The cheeses in this book have a silky, rich mouthfeel that is absolutely decadent. I've served these cheeses to carnivores and vegans alike and the reaction is always celebratory. In fact, the title of this book comes from something my friend Daryl Wein once said after he tried a spread of Cashew Bleu, Camembert, and Smoked Gouda. He actually exclaimed, "This cheese is nuts!"

You can also be assured that plant-based cheese is good for your body too. That heavy feeling, indigestion, even stomach pain that so many of us experience after eating dairy? Completely gone. To be able to enjoy the full-bodied creamy flavor of a Gorgonzola sauce over pasta and feel great afterward is truly a divine experience. All of the recipes in this book are made with pure, nourishing ingredients—straight from nature.

This cheese is good for your taste buds and good for your body. But as important, eating plant-based cheeses is also an acknowledgment that we will no longer turn a blind eye to the horrors of the industrialized meat and dairy industries, nor will we ignore the impact our food choices have on our health and our planet.

DAIRY AND DISEASE

It's crucial that we understand that dairy is making us sick. Dairy has been linked to a host of health conditions including heart disease, cancer, allergies, and digestive problems. The problems seem to be with A1 beta-casein in particular. I healed a large cyst in my neck with the support of the eastern Indian science of Ayurveda, which prescribes warm milk as medicine and medicated ghee as part of the healing treatment. But the sacred milk revered in Ayurvedic medicine is not your ordinary cow's milk. According to revered Vedic monk His Holiness Swami Vidyadhishananda, the milk prescribed as medicine has its origins in the indigenous Brahman cow, which produces milk that is made of A2 beta-casein and not the A1 beta-casein widely found in processed milk products today. A1 beta-casein is the culprit in many health imbalances.

SACRED COW

I hear from many people that while they understand why one would not want to eat meat and participate in the violence perpetrated against animals within the industrialized meat industry, they find it a more abstract concept to understand what could be harmful in consuming cheese, butters, and ice creams made from cow's milk and goat milk. Most people sincerely believe that cows and goats are not harmed in any way by being raised for their milk. What many of us are not aware of is that the dairy industry is brutalizing cows, using inhumane practices such as containing them in tight quarters, where they

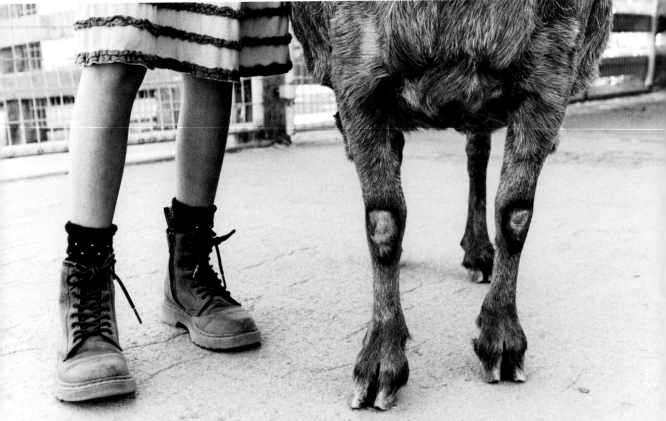

stand in their own feces. The cows are injected with high levels of hormones to keep them producing milk for an extended period of time, and after their milk dries up, the cows are sold for slaughter to the meat industry. So-called free-range conditions are far removed from a cow grazing peacefully in a green pasture. If we could witness the brutality that is inflicted onto these deeply feeling animals, we would not want to support these harmful acts by consuming milk products. Most of us have no idea what full-grown cows look like since they are usually killed early in adolescence.

In their natural state, cows are majestic, conscious, and beautiful beings. In the ancient Vedas of yogic tradition, the cow represents Mother, a caretaker of people and Earth, and is revered for her sacred energy. With each meal, we are presented with an opportunity to practice nonviolence, or what the yogis call *ahimsa*, in order to live more conscious, connected, and meaningful lives. Goodness knows we have enough violence already on this planet; it's time we take compassionate action in our lives.

MOTHER EARTH

We are all intrinsically connected to this magnificent planet we are riding on and our very lives depend on her health and well-being. Eating plant-based cheeses is a powerful action you can take today that will immediately have a positive impact on the environment. Did you know that it takes 1,000 gallons of water to produce one gallon of milk? With global warming conditions evident in our own backyards, the responsibility is weighing on us to take meaningful action. By choosing plant-based cheeses on your plate, you will reduce your *footprint* far more than environmental gains experienced from riding your bike, using alternative energies, recycling, taking shorter showers, or even driving an electric car. In addition, embracing a plant-based lifestyle will make a dramatic and immediate positive impact on your own physical health and it will connect you to your life purpose. All of us were created from a divine blueprint to play a very specific part in life's symphony. The world needs you to be more of who you are.

WE ARE DEEPLY AFFECTED BY WHAT WE EAT

In these uncertain times, with so much violence happening all over the world, we are often rendered feeling helpless, hopeless, sad, and angry. We must be careful that we do not turn to habitual eating patterns with absolutely no awareness of what we are putting in our mouths. We must understand that If an animal has been brutalized and then slaughtered even if in a so-called free-range environment, this energy of violence becomes a part of us when taken into the body temple. As feeling and caring humans, we can all agree that there is too much violence in the world today and we need to take actions in our own lives to lessen this anti-life part of our world. We are not separate from other creatures on this earth, both animals and humans. We are also not separate from this planet, or what we eat. Fortunately, there is something we all can do right now. We can make a meaningful difference by choosing plants on our plates at every meal. Every time we eat plant-based, we refrain from participating in adding more violence, harm, and suffering into our bodies and into the human collective.

CHEESE THAT EVEN CHEESE HATERS WILL LOVE: When I lived in Paris, I bought a wheel of cheese to bring home for dinner. On the subway, I was sitting next to a man who I thought smelled disgusting! I had to cover my nose as I counted the seconds to my stop so I could switch trains. When I settled into my seat on the next train, the "degulas" smell again filled my sinus cavity. I was horrified as the realization that it was me who was creating the stench sunk in! As the train pulled into the station, I threw open the door and ran as fast as I could to my apartment. I leaped up the winding staircase, slammed the door open, and began throwing off my clothes as I raced into the shower. I washed my hair vigorously and used soap on every inch of my entire body. I was relieved that thankfully the smell was gone. Later that night my friend Sophie came home, walked in the kitchen and smelled the cheese I had purchased and she said, "*Qui achete cette fromage? Elle peut marcher toute seul!* Translation: "Who bought this cheese? It can walk by itself!"

One big difference between plant-based cheese and traditional cheese is that it has a much fresher taste and smell. No smelly, pungent cheeses here. I don't use molds in my cheeses at all (more on that on page 28). So for cheese haters who are sensitive to what I like to call "smelly, old tennis shoe" cheese (or even cheese that is only a little bit stinky!), trying these recipes will open up a whole new world to them.

I've seen this firsthand. My son Tyler has despised cheese since he was a baby. When he was as young as two years old, if someone near him was eating cheese, he could smell it and wanted it moved away from him. My niece Maggie is also not a cheese fan. But *This Cheese Is Nuts!* has won them over!

CREATIVITY AND CHANGE STARTS IN YOUR KITCHEN

How could it be possible to create creamy-tasting cheese without using milk or dairy? What I've learned is that when we open ourselves up to new ways of approaching food and we are willing to experiment, we can let go of thinking there's only "one way" and truly innovate. There is creativity waiting to be channeled through all of us. This is a powerful life lesson too. If the problem exists, then so does the answer to that problem. If we allow ourselves to have the courage to let go of what is outdated and no longer serves our greatest potential as human beings, then we will receive the guidance.

Making nut cheeses confirms for me, without exception, that plant-based is still the easiest, fastest, tastiest, and healthiest way to cook, eat, and live, I hope you enjoy these recipes, and, most of all, I hope that you'll use them as the starting point for your own exciting and unique creations!

A BALANCED APPROACH: Keep in mind that the creamy cheeses in this cookbook should be part of a balanced plant-based diet. Enjoy them as a garnish or a sauce to meals that are teeming with healthy leafy greens, fresh organic farmers market fair, and whole fruits and veggies. If you are overweight or have heart disease, you should opt for recipes in the nut-free and dairy-free chapters as much as possible.

BEFORE YOU START: TOOLS, INGREDIENTS & A FEW WORDS ABOUT TECHNIQUE

Once you get the hang of the process, you will see that making plant-based cheeses is relatively easy. Plant-based cheeses are much simpler to prepare than dairy cheeses! Making vegan cheese also opens you up to a whole new world of wonderful flavors, textures, and aromas. The possibilities for your creations are truly endless.

Many of the cheeses in this book take only twenty minutes to make. Others require longer aging or setting time but don't require much hands-on time from you. I've included a few multistep recipes that are great fun to try when you have a little more time. But most of my recipes are designed for you to be able to prepare and enjoy every day.

ESSENTIAL EQUIPMENT

Making delicious vegan cheese at home is incredibly easy once you get the hang of it. Many cheeses can be made with a food processor. But in order to to take your plant-based diet to the next level, a few key items will make your cheese creations go easier with superior results in taste, and texture.

VITAMIX

I definitely recommend investing in a Vitamix (model 7500 or a higher model). A regular blender just can't blend nuts as well and create the smooth consistency that a Vitamix can. If you don't use a Vitamix, you'll likely have chunks of nuts throughout, or the texture will be too grainy and you may not have a pleasing result.

FOOD PROCESSOR

This versatile machine is handy for preparing fresh coconut and for many of my quick spreads. I like the professional series KitchenAid model.

DEHYDRATOR

A dehydrator is certainly not essential if you want to stick to the "Quick 'Form' Cheeses" and most of the sauces and spreads. But for more depth of flavor and that elusive "aged" quality, a dehydrator works wonders. I like to use the Sedona Dehydrator.

If the idea of using a dehydrator seems daunting, I promise you, it isn't difficult! As a mother, wife, chef, author, and healer, I need to streamline my cooking, and a dehydrator works with my busy lifestyle.

COCO-JACK

This is a handy tool that will open young coconuts safely and quickly.

CHEF'S TORCH

Will take your crème brûlée to the next level. You can get one online for under $20.

CHEESE MOLDS AND SPRINGFORM PANS

The best molds and pans to use are aluminum or stainless steel in the following sizes: 4 x 2-inch round, 4.5 x 1.5-inch springform, 6 x 3.5 x 2-inch rectangular. You can find these online.

FINE CHEESECLOTH

It's essential to use a high-quality, fine cheesecloth when you are making these recipes. You can find it online or in a gourmet kitchen store.

SMALL AND MEDIUM RUBBER SPATULAS

You need two small rubber spatulas on hand to scrape your cheese out of the Vitamix and food processor. A medium-size rubber spatula is ideal for stirring warm cheeses.

ICE CREAM SCOOPER

This is very helpful for scraping the cheese from cheesecloth or from your cheese mold.

PANTRY STAPLES

With these ingredients on hand, you'll be able to put together my plant-based cheese recipes in a snap. Most of the ingredients will be familiar to you and easy to find at any local grocer. A few are more specialized, but they are still easy to find.

NUTS!

Nuts are the star of plant-based cheeses (although in "Nut-Free Cheeses & Spreads," I do offer recipes for cheeses using a base of sunflower seeds, white beans, chickpeas, and tofu for those with nut allergies).

CASHEWS

Many of my cheeses are made with cashews. Cashews always deliver! Note when you are buying cashews that those sold as raw cashews are not really raw. Cashews are roasted to remove their toxic outer shell, which has properties similar to poison ivy. This is why you can't sprout cashews. They can be re-roasted like other nuts, or activated using a dehydrator.

While I love using cashews in my plant-based cheeses, it's also important not to create an imbalance by overeating one type of nut, so I've also developed many recipes using other nuts.

MACADAMIA NUTS

Macadamia nuts are delicious, but they have a grainy texture. I don't use them as much because they are expensive. Feel free to experiment and use them as a blend with another nut.

PINE NUTS

Pine nuts are great to use in a blend or in pesto. They are the least nutritious nut, so they are good for bringing in some variation, but they are not the best nut to use as a staple.

ALMONDS

Almonds are wonderful in vegan cheeses, but note that you must blanch them and remove the skins in many recipes. This is well worth the effort! Be aware that vegan cheeses made with almonds require more oil than other cheeses because almonds are not as fatty.

A NOTE ON BUYING ALMONDS: While it is true that almonds require a lot of water to produce, this usage pales in comparison to the astronomical water usage, land decimation, ocean dead zones, methane gas, and animal brutality that result from meat and dairy consumption.

NOTE: The most efficient quantity of nuts for every recipe is 2 cups. The reason for this is if you use less, the blade in the Vitamix will not be able to blend it properly. If you double a recipe, which I often do, do not double the salt or liquid smoke quantity. Add only the amount for one batch and then add more to taste.

OTHER INGREDIENTS

REFINED COCONUT OIL

Coconut oil is an extremely healthy fat for the body. It is derived from the most sacred fruit on the planet. The Coconut is the embodiment of Mother Gaia's milk. Coconut oil has a slew of superfood benefits and a divine energy vibration. It melts in your mouth, lubricates your joints and intestinal tract, and it's even a wonderful lotion!

I use refined coconut oil rather than regular coconut oil in many of my recipes because it is unscented. I have used regular coconut oil in some of the ricottas and the mozzarella and I love it, but you can taste the coconut flavor.

If you are overweight or have heart disease, it is a good idea to consume less fat, even healthy fats. Start by cutting the oil in my recipes in half and work up to using only a quarter of the full amount.

BETA-CAROTENE

My absolute favorite way to add color and healing properties to cheese is by using beta-carotene. Yes, there are ingredients such as turmeric and annatto, made from the seeds of the achiote, that can also add color. But with turmeric you have to deal with the bitter taste, and annatto is not as easy to find. Beta-carotene capsules will last a long time stored in your refrigerator. Add one to four drops to get your favorite, deliciously golden shade.

MODIFIED TAPIOCA STARCH

This is not the same thing as tapioca starch. Modified tapioca starch is an excellent natural thickening agent. I learned to add this ingredient to my cheeses by studying the ingredients in packaged vegan cheese. You can find it online.

AGAR-AGAR POWDER

Agar is a red algae and a unique vegetable protein source. I use agar-agar powder or agar-agar flakes in my cheese recipes. The flakes are more expensive, as you need to use more of them to achieve the same result. It's my favorite ingredient to use to firm up the texture of plant-based block cheeses. It is important to find organic sources, preferably from the Atlantic. While it will never make your cheese firm enough to grate, you can create a sliceable cheese. Also, if you spread the warm cooked "form" cheese straight from the pot onto bread for a cheese sandwich (rather than setting it in molds), it produces a warm, thick, "melt in your mouth" texture.

> **A NOTE ON KAPPA CARRAGEENAN:** Kappa carrageenan, a red seaweed that comes from Morocco, can be used as a thickener or firming agent in vegan cooking. But I've found that it can cause problems for people with digestive issues and so I've chosen not to use it in my recipes. Agar-agar and modified tapioca starch work just as well to harden vegan cheeses.

APPLE CIDER VINEGAR

Apple cider vinegar is an all-time favorite alkalizing superfood.

LACTIC ACID

A natural acid made from sugar beets.

LEMON JUICE

Lemon juice is the freshest and simplest way to add an aged flavor to your cheeses. Also alkalizing, it is very healing for the body.

ACIDOPHILUS

Acidophilus is a probiotic and the key to nut-cheese nirvana. In the early days, I experimented with various quantities and strain counts of acidophilus, as well as dehydrating times. After some trial and error, I have found that using 1/2 to 1 capsule of a 3-billion-active-culture strain and dehydrating the nut cheese for 24 hours is the magic recipe for a perfectly aged taste. You can find acidophilus in the health food section of your market.

IRISH MOSS

Irish moss is a seaweed variety that thickens beautifully. You must take care to wash it repeatedly to remove the sand and sea smell before using it. Soaking it overnight and emulsifying it are key steps. Also be sure to use the exact quantity called for in the recipes. If you happen to add a bit too much, it may add a slight "mermaid" taste to your cheese.

AQUAFABA

The secret ingredient of every gourmet vegan chef, this is just a fancy name for the liquid inside a can of garbanzo beans (there's usually about 3/4 cup of liquid inside one can). You can make it yourself, but why would you? It is so easy to use right out of the can. I created a garbanzo cheese recipe so you can make good use of the leftover garbanzo beans (see Quick Chickpea Cheesy Spread, page 170).

REJUVELAC

A probiotic made from grain. It will age similar to acidolphilus. You can find it at natural markets.

SALT

Celtic sea salt, Himalayan salt, and truffle salt are my favorites. Perfect quantities of these varieties will take your cheese to the next level. Indian black salt will give you a sulfur taste that is reminiscent of boiled eggs.

NUTRITIONAL YEAST

Loaded with vitamin B_{12} and other B vitamins, this is a delicious and nutritious way to up the cheesy flavor in your plant-based cheeses. Feel free to increase the quantity if you are so inspired.

MISO PASTE

Using miso paste is another great way to add flavor to your cheeses. At a specialty Japanese market, you can find many varieties of organic miso paste, such as barley miso paste and brown rice miso paste. The taste is superior to what you can find in regular markets. Chickpea miso paste is a standard favorite and is easily found at health food stores.

LIQUID SMOKE

It may surprise you to learn that liquid smoke is made from natural ingredients. I love to use it in my Smoked Almond Cheddar Spread (page 33) and my Smoked Gouda (page 64), which is always a party favorite! Treat liquid smoke like salt when doubling recipes—only add enough for one batch and then add more to taste. You can find this specialty item online and in gourmet food stores.

DOES IT MELT LIKE REGULAR CHEESE?: Some years ago, I tried out a brand of shredded almond cheese and melted it over a pile of nachos. The taste was okay, but when I went to clean the pan, no matter how hard I scrubbed, I could not remove the melted cheese from the serving tray. As I soaked and scrubbed some more, I reflected on what had happened to the constitution of this cheese when it melted and also realized that this cement-hard substance was what my body was trying to process and digest at the same moment. Well, that can't be good, I thought.

Since that day, we have been pouring a warm nacho cheese sauce (Classic Cashew Cheese Sauce, page 54) over our Torre de Nachos recipe from *The Plantpower Way*. It is delectably delicious, so much so that it begs sighs of delight out of the mouths of my family. We also started using it on pizzas we prepare at home with blackened tomato sauce, and veggies like olives, mushrooms, and peppers. Right out of the oven, we smother the pizzas with warm Classic Cashew Cheese Sauce and topped them with herbs and fresh arugula tossed in lemon and olive oil. Pizza has never tasted so incredibly delicious.

I've done a lot of research on how to achieve a "grate-able" cheese to replace store-bought shredded cheese. Many plant-based recipes use kappa carrageenan, a red seaweed from Morocco, as a firming ingredient. I experimented with kappa carrageenan and found it didn't work very well (more on that on page 25). And in the end, my Classic Cashew Cheese Sauce always wins.

TECHNIQUE TIPS

QUICK CHEESES

It's easy to tweak the texture and flavor of these cheeses to suit your taste. When making easy, quick cheeses in the bowl of a food processor, feel free to adjust the consistency by adding the liquid in the recipe 1 tablespoon at a time. You can also add more cheese flavor by adding nutritional yeast 1 tablespoon at a time.

FORM CHEESES

Making form cheeses, such as cheddar (Smoked Almond Cheddar Spread, page 33), Provolone (page 73), Smoked Gouda (page 64), and Mozzarella Balls in Brine (page 67) is one of the trickiest techniques in this book. Begin by blending everything in your Vitamix except the acid—that is, everything but the lemon juice, acidophilus, or apple cider vinegar (you will wait to add the acid until the very end of the cooking process, after you remove the pan from the heat). The difficult part of the process is cooking the mixture on the stove. The first five times you try this method, use a thermometer and cook over low heat. Stir the mixture constantly until it is done, making sure you get underneath the thermometer stick. If you start to see lumps, remove the pan from the heat and start to whisk the ingredients with a wire whisk. Then return it to the stove over low heat and stir again. The cheese is done when it has reached about 145 degrees F and you can see it pull away clean from the sides of the pan as you are stirring it. Turn off the heat and add the acid if the recipe calls for it, stir to incorporate, and then pour the mixture into cheese molds (or drop it into brine).

A WORD ON MOLDS AND RINDS: I experimented by adding molds with the intention of setting up rinds that are characteristic of traditional aged cheeses such as Camembert, Brie, and Triple Cream. Twelve hours after opening the package of mold that I added to my test cheese, my sinuses became inflamed. Later I experienced sunken eyes and cystic breakouts after sampling a cheese with a moldy rind. This made me question whether those of us committed to experiencing true health would find it in our best interest to be ingesting mold in the first place.

I decided not to present rinds in this book. The tastes of my Camembert (Cashew Camembert, page 88), Brie (Cashew Brie, page 87), and Triple Cream (page 91) speak for themselves. While in traditional cheese making, the rind may enhance the flavor, in plant-based cheeses I did not find it significant enough to warrant mold in the body.

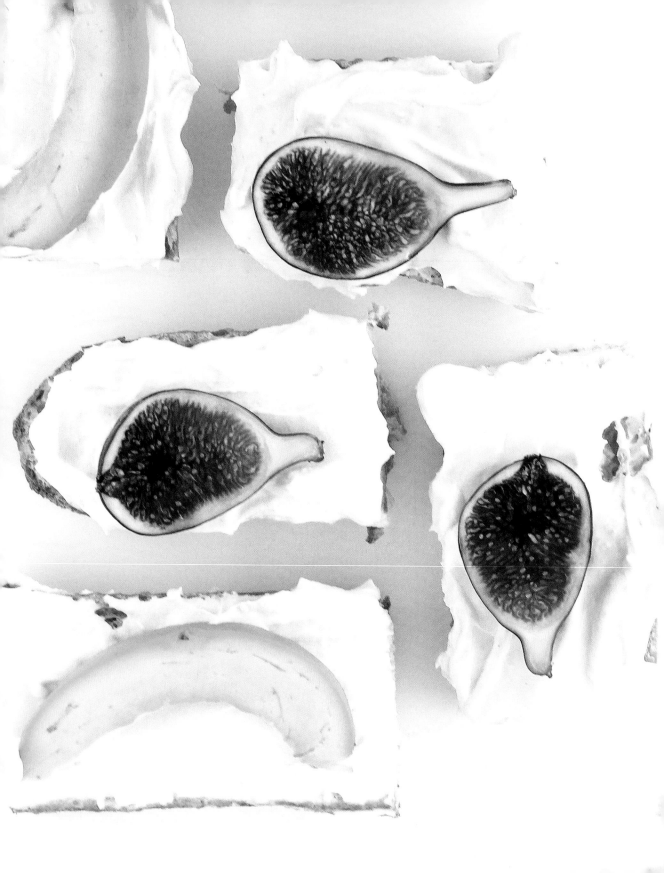

CHEESE SPREADS & SAUCES

SMOKED ALMOND CHEDDAR SPREAD

ROASTED CASHEW APPLE SPREAD

ARTICHOKE SPINACH SPREAD

BOTIJA OLIVE ROSEMARY CHEESE SPREAD

CHICORY ALMOND CHEESY SPREAD

CLASSIC FONDUE

CLASSIC HOLLANDAISE SAUCE

CLASSIC CREAM CHEESE

COCONUT CASHEW CREAM CHEESE

3-HERB MACADAMIA–PINE NUT CHEESY PESTO

WARM QUESO FRESCO

CLASSIC CASHEW CHEESE SAUCE

ANCHO CHILI NACHO CHEESE

SMOKED ALMOND CHEDDAR SPREAD

My number-one all-time favorite quick cheese! Start here and you'll be WINNING. ■ **SERVES 4 TO 6**

2 cups raw almonds

½ to ¾ cup pimientos from a jar, plus ½ to ¾ cup packing liquid

¼ cup nutritional yeast

1¾ teaspoons smoked sea salt

1 teaspoon garlic powder

EASY PRE-PREP:
Rinse the almonds well. Place them in water in a medium bowl. Cover and refrigerate overnight.

1. Drain the almonds. In the bowl of a food processor, place the almonds, pimientos, nutritional yeast, salt, garlic powder, and ¼ cup pimiento liquid. Process until the mixture is well incorporated.

2. Remove the lid and test the cheese for texture and salt content. If you want a smoother spread, add more pimiento liquid in small increments and process again. Add more salt if needed.

3. Serve with crackers and fresh pears.

ROASTED CASHEW APPLE SPREAD

This lovely spread would be perfect to take on a picnic in the French countryside. It's a sweet cheese that travels well. Serve it with a full-bodied organic pomegranate kombucha. ■ MAKES 1½ CUPS

1 cup cashews

2 cups packed fresh spinach

1 cup packed dried apples

¼ teaspoon Celtic sea salt

2 tablespoons nutritional yeast

2 tablespoons filtered water, plus more as needed

1. Preheat the oven to 350 degrees F.

2. Roast the cashews on a rimmed baking sheet for 10 minutes or until golden brown.

3. While the cashews are roasting, soak the apples in 1 cup boiling water for 10 minutes.

4. In the bowl of a food processor, place the spinach first, then top with the cashews, apples, salt, nutritional yeast, and the water.

5. Process until the mixture balls up on one side of the bowl. Add more water 1 tablespoon at a time to reach a smooth, spreadable cheese.

6. Transfer to a beautiful serving bowl and enjoy with your favorite crackers. Voilà!

ARTICHOKE SPINACH SPREAD

Finally, a delicious artichoke appetizer that is incredibly delicious and healthy. Another great cheese spread for a brunch or eating outdoors, it travels wonderfully. I serve this at room temperature, but if you want it saucy and warm like a dip, replace the cashews in this recipe with Warm Queso Fresco (page 53). ■ MAKES 1 CUP

1 cup cashews

1 teaspoon olive oil

1 cup fresh spinach

1 tablespoon nutritional yeast

1 cup roasted artichoke hearts from a jar

1 teaspoon lemon juice

1/2 teaspoon Celtic sea salt

1. Preheat the oven to 350 degrees F.

2. Roast the cashews on a rimmed baking sheet for 10 minutes or until golden brown.

3. In a medium saucepan over medium-low heat, add the olive oil and spinach and sauté for 2 minutes or until the spinach is wilted but still bright green.

4. In the bowl of a food processor, place the roasted cashews, nutritional yeast, artichoke hearts, lemon juice, and salt.

5. Pulse until the cheese forms a ball on the side of the bowl.

6. Add in the cooked spinach and pulse a few times until it is incorporated.

7. Serve with chips, crackers, or toast.

BOTIJA OLIVE ROSEMARY CHEESE SPREAD

Botija olives are dried gourmet olives found in specialty stores. They have a subtler, milder flavor than most olives, and they are the best to use in this recipe. Roasting the pine nuts first really brings out their nutty flavor and gives the spread a beautiful caramel color. Serve it on Tuscan crackers or use it on a roasted veggie pizza. ■ MAKES 1 CUP

1 cup pine nuts

1 teaspoon fresh chopped rosemary

3 tablespoons nutritional yeast

1/2 teaspoon Celtic sea salt

6 black botija olives

1. Preheat the oven to 350 degrees F.

2. Roast the pine nuts on a rimmed baking sheet for 8 minutes or until caramel in color.

3. In the bowl of a food processor, place the roasted pine nuts, rosemary, nutritional yeast, salt, and 3 olives and pulse until the mixture is well incorporated.

4. Transfer to a clay serving bowl and garnish with the remaining 3 olives.

CHICORY ALMOND CHEESY SPREAD

This exotic-tasting spread begs for India. Serve with naan and your favorite chutney. Chicory root is a digestive aid and was consumed in ancient times for liver purification.

■ **MAKES 2 CUPS**

2 cups almonds

4 tablespoons nutritional yeast

2 teaspoons chicory root

½ teaspoon salt

½ teaspoon cinnamon, plus more for garnish

1 tablespoon brown rice miso paste

1 tablespoon balsamic vinegar

2 teaspoons refined coconut oil

½ to ¾ cup filtered water

EASY PRE-PREP:
Rinse the almonds well. Place them in filtered water in a small bowl. Cover and refrigerate overnight.

1. Preheat the oven to 350 degrees F.

2. Drain the almonds and roast them on a rimmed baking sheet for 10 minutes.

3. In the bowl of a food processor, place the almonds, nutritional yeast, chicory root, salt, cinnamon, miso, balsamic vinegar, coconut oil, and ½ cup water.

4. Process until the mixture is well incorporated and the mixture balls up on one side of the bowl.

5. Add more water, 1 tablespoon at a time, until the desired consistency is reached.

6. Using your hands, mold the spread into a disk shape or transfer into a serving dish. Dust the top with cinnamon and serve.

CLASSIC FONDUE

I adore fondue! There isn't anything better than friends gathering around a warm savory dish après-ski. Surprisingly Swiss-like in flavor, it might just transport you to Chamonix. ■ MAKES 2 CUPS

2 cups raw cashews

1 garlic clove

½ teaspoon mustard powder

⅛ teaspoon nutmeg

1 teaspoon onion powder

½ teaspoon white pepper

1 teaspoon Celtic sea salt, plus more to taste

1 tablespoon nutritional yeast

1 tablespoon chickpea miso paste

¼ cup refined coconut oil

¼ cup modified tapioca starch

1 teaspoon saffron threads dissolved in ½ cup filtered hot water

1½ cups filtered hot water

1 tablespoon sherry vinegar or white wine vinegar

EASY PRE-PREP:
Place the cashews in filtered water in a small bowl. Cover and refrigerate overnight.

1. Drain the cashews. In the bowl of a Vitamix, place the cashews, garlic, mustard powder, nutmeg, onion powder, pepper, salt, vinegar, nutritional yeast, miso, coconut oil, modified tapioca starch, and saffron threads and soaking water, plus 1½ cups more water.

2. Blend on medium speed for about 30 seconds. Increase to high speed and continue blending for 90 seconds more.

3. Place the mixture in a small saucepan and heat through, **stirring constantly**. Keep the flame on low, as if you heat the cheese too fast, it will become lumpy. If this happens, turn off the flame and whisk the mixture until smooth. Then begin again. The cheese is done when it starts to pull clean from the edge of the pan as you stir. The first few times you try it, you can use a thermometer and heat the mixture to 145 degrees F.

4. Turn off the flame, fold in the sherry vinegar, and adjust salt to taste. Pour into a fondue serving dish.

5. Serve with skewered fresh apples, pears, celery, butternut squash, fermented sourdough cubes, or gluten-free bread cubes.

CLASSIC HOLLANDAISE SAUCE

I'm proud to present this perfect brunch sauce to smother my N'Eggs Bennie (see N'Eggs Bennie with Hollandaise Sauce and Coconut Bacon, page 148). ■ **MAKES 2 CUPS**

1 cup almonds

1 cup cashews

2 tablespoons fresh lemon juice

½ cup vegan butter

1 teaspoon Celtic sea salt

¼ teaspoon freshly ground pepper

5 tablespoons nutritional yeast

2 tablespoons black truffle oil

¼ teaspoon fresh or ground turmeric

2 cups boiling water

EASY PRE-PREP:

1. Soak the almonds for at least 8 hours in filtered water. To sprout them, rinse the almonds with water twice a day for the next 48 hours. You can store them covered with a piece of cheesecloth in a cool, dry place. But make sure you drain the water from them completely each time you rinse them. Or, if desired, you can skip the sprouting step and just use soaked almonds. Your cheese will still be delicious.

2. Soak the cashews overnight in filtered water in the fridge.

---

1. Bring 4 cups of water to a boil in a medium saucepan over medium-high heat. Add the almonds and blanch them for 1 minute. Drain the almonds in a colander and remove the skins with your fingers (you can compost the skins). Drain the cashews in a colander.

2. In the bowl of a Vitamix, place the almonds, cashews, lemon juice, vegan butter, salt, pepper, nutritional yeast, truffle oil, turmeric, and 2 cups boiling water. Blend on high speed for 2 minutes. Pour over N'Eggs Bennie.

CLASSIC CREAM CHEESE

Great on bagels, toast, or any of your favorite gluten-free breads! ■ **MAKES 2 CUPS**

2 cups raw cashews

½ teaspoon refined coconut oil, for greasing the pans

¾ cup aquafaba (liquid from canned garbanzo beans)

½ capsule acidophilus (3-billion-active-culture strain)

EASY PRE-PREP:
Place the cashews in filtered water in a small bowl. Cover and refrigerate overnight.

1. Lightly oil two 4-inch springform pans with coconut oil.

2. Drain the cashews. In the bowl of a Vitamix, place the cashews, aquafaba, and acidolphilus.

3. Blend on medium speed, increasing to high speed, using the plunger to evenly distribute the mixture until smooth. Transfer the cheese to the prepared springform pans, smoothing the tops with a rubber spatula.

4. Cut out a round of parchment paper that just fits the springform pan openings. (You don't have to cover it securely, as often the mixture will rise slightly beyond the top of the pan; this is fine.) Place the springform pans in the dehydrator and dehydrate at 90 degrees F for 24 hours.

5. Using an ice cream scooper, remove the inside of the cheese and transfer it to a glass storage container. Refrigerate overnight.

6. Spread on your favorite breads.

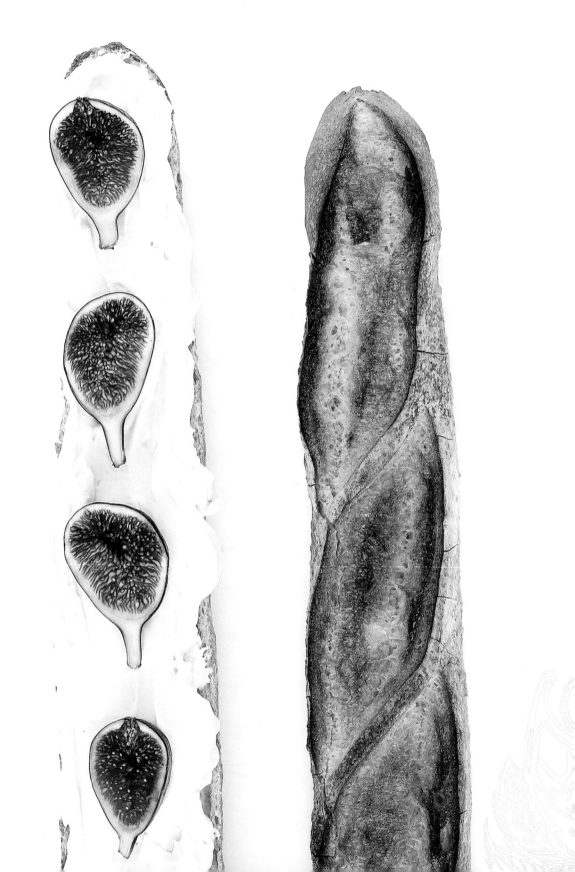

COCONUT CASHEW CREAM CHEESE

This tropical combination makes for a versatile cheese base that you can spread on almost everything in creation. ■ **MAKES TWO 4-INCH ROUND MOLDS**

2 cups raw cashews

2 tablespoons coconut oil, plus more for greasing the cheese molds

2 cups fresh coconut meat from a brown coconut (do not substitute with coconut flakes)

3/4 cup aquafaba (liquid from canned garbanzo beans)

EASY PRE-PREP:
Place the cashews in filtered water in a small bowl. Cover and refrigerate overnight.

1. Lightly oil two 4-inch cheese molds with coconut oil and line with fine cheesecloth, leaving extra to drape over the tops.

2. Drain the cashews. In the bowl of a Vitamix, place the cashews, coconut oil, coconut, and aquafaba and blend for 2½ minutes or until smooth. For a very smooth texture, really make an effort to work with the plunger to distribute the cheese evenly so it blends properly. It's only 1 or 2 minutes of using your muscles and it is well worth the effort!

3. Fold the mixture into the molds. Smooth the tops out with a rubber spatula and cover with rounds of parchment cut to fit the tops of the molds.

4. Place the cheese molds in the dehydrator and dehydrate at 90 degrees F for 24 hours.

5. Transfer to the fridge and refrigerate overnight to set up.

6. Using an ice cream scooper, spoon the cream cheese from the molds into a small serving bowl, leaving the harder rind behind.

7. Spread on your favorite, bread, baguettes, or crackers.

3-HERB MACADAMIA—PINE NUT CHEESY PESTO

Fresh, vibrant, and lively, this garden pesto is perfect over pasta or spaghetti squash noodles, or as a spread on your panini. Add small increments of water until it reaches the desired consistency. ■ **MAKES 2 CUPS**

1 cup salted macadamia nuts

1 cup pine nuts

2 cups packed fresh basil

1/2 cup fresh spearmint

1/2 cup fresh oregano

2 tablespoons nutritional yeast

1/2 teaspoon Himalayan salt

I tablespoon filtered water, plus more as needed

1. Preheat the oven to 350 degrees F.

2. Place the macadamia nuts and pine nuts on a rimmed baking sheet and roast in the oven for 8 minutes or until golden brown.

3. In the bowl of a food processor, place the basil, spearmint, and oregano. Add the roasted nuts and nutritional yeast on top.

4. Pulse until the mixture is mealy and the oil releases from the nuts. Add water, 1 tablespoon at a time, until the desired consistency is reached.

5. Serve over any kind of pasta or use as a sandwich spread.

WARM QUESO FRESCO

This mild, sweeter cheese sauce is a welcome cool taste in spicy Mexican dishes. Pour it over tacos or enchiladas, or use it as a topping for a great bowl of black bean soup. Feel free to double the recipe. Just don't double the salt! ■ MAKES 2¼ CUPS

1 cup raw cashews

1 cup pine nuts

1 tablespoon chickpea miso paste

1 tablespoon refined coconut oil

2 tablespoons nutritional yeast

½ teaspoon Celtic sea salt

1 tablespoon fresh lemon juice

2 garlic cloves

¼ to ¾ cup filtered hot water

EASY PRE-PREP:
Place the cashews in filtered water in a small bowl. Cover and refrigerate overnight.

1. Drain the cashews. In the pitcher of a Vitamix, place the cashews, pine nuts, miso, coconut oil, nutritional yeast, salt, lemon juice, garlic, and ¼ cup of hot water.

2. Blend on medium speed, using the plunger to evenly distribute the mixture.

3. Add more hot water, ¼ cup at a time, to reach the desired consistency. Adjust the seasonings to taste.

CLASSIC CASHEW CHEESE SAUCE

I've never found a store-bought vegan cheese that melts well. Some are so gooey that they become gross, while others don't really melt and have a grainy texture to them.

Many moons ago, we stopped melting cheese and instead opted for this warm cashew cheese sauce. This recipe is an absolute innovation in plant-based cheese and one of the easiest cheeses to prepare. It makes an off-the-charts delicious replacement for the hard, melted cheeses of old. ■ MAKES 2 CUPS

2 cups raw cashews

2 tablespoons chickpea miso paste

1 tablespoon coconut oil

¼ cup nutritional yeast

½ teaspoon Celtic sea salt

1 teaspoon fresh lemon juice

1 cup boiling water, plus more as needed

EASY PRE-PREP:
Place the cashews in filtered water in a small bowl. Cover and refrigerate overnight.

1. Drain the cashews. In the pitcher of a Vitamix, place the cashews, miso, coconut oil, nutritional yeast, salt, lemon juice, and 1 cup water.

2. Blend on medium speed, using the plunger to evenly distribute the mixture.

3. Add additional hot water, ¼ cup at a time, until the desired consistency is reached. Adjust the seasonings to taste.

4. Pour this sauce over nachos or over veggie pizza fresh out of the oven, or use it to smother Blackened Cauliflower (page 143) or any other cooked veggies.

ANCHO CHILI NACHO CHEESE

For die-hard Tex-Mex lovers. A delicious warm dip for your organic blue chip.

■ **MAKES 2¼ CUPS**

1 cup raw cashews

1 cup pine nuts

1 tablespoon chickpea miso paste

1 tablespoon refined coconut oil

2 tablespoons nutritional yeast

½ teaspoon Celtic sea salt

1 tablespoon fresh lemon juice

2 garlic cloves

1½ teaspoons ancho chili powder

¼ teaspoon garlic powder

⅛ teaspoon cayenne pepper

½ teaspoon apple cider vinegar

½ cup boiling water

1½ sprigs of fresh cilantro

EASY PRE-PREP:
Place the cashews in filtered water in a small bowl. Cover and refrigerate overnight.

1. Drain the cashews. In the pitcher of a Vitamix, place the cashews, pine nuts, miso, coconut oil, nutritional yeast, salt, lemon juice, garlic, ancho chili powder, garlic powder, cayenne, vinegar, and the water.

2. Blend on medium speed, using the plunger to evenly distribute the mixture.

3. Add more hot water, ¼ cup at a time, to reach the desired consistency. Adjust the seasonings to taste. Garnish with fresh cilantro.

QUICK "FORM" CHEESES

CASHEW CHEDDAR

SHARP CHEDDAR

SMOKED GOUDA

MOZZARELLA BALLS IN BRINE

CASHEW-ALMOND MOZZARELLA

PROVOLONE

EYE OF RA MASCARPONE

CASHEW TRUFFLE PARMESAN

CASHEW CHEDDAR

A divine, melt-in-your-mouth sliceable golden cheese gift from the Gods, this "form" cheese has a gooey consistency without being gross like many store-bought vegan cheeses. When it's still warm, it's like a spreadable melted cheese. ■ **MAKES ONE 4.5 x 1-INCH ROUND**

1 cup raw cashews

1 cup filtered water

1 teaspoon Himalayan salt

¼ cup modified tapioca starch

Beta-carotene squeezed from 2 gel caps

¼ cup refined coconut oil, plus more for greasing the pan

1½ teaspoons agar-agar powder

EASY PRE-PREP:
Place the cashews in filtered water in a small bowl. Cover and refrigerate overnight.

1. Drain the cashews. In the pitcher of a Vitamix, place the cashews, water, modified tapioca starch, beta-carotene, coconut oil, and agar-agar powder.

2. Blend on high speed until smooth.

3. Oil a 4.5 x 1-inch round springform pan with coconut oil.

4. Transfer the cashew mixture to a saucepan and heat on medium-low, **stirring continuously,** until it becomes thick and cheese-like in consistency. (You can use a thermometer and heat the mixture to about 145 degrees F. See page 28 for tips on this technique.)

5. At this stage, you can spread this warm, thick cheese onto toasted bread for a delicious sandwich. or you can fold the cheese into the prepared mold .and set it aside to cool.

6. Refrigerate the cheese overnight to set up.

7. Run a knife around the inside edge of the mold. Release the buckle on the springform pan and, using the flat edge of a large knife, release the cheese from the bottom metal round.

8. Transfer to a cutting board. Using a sharp knife, slice the cheese and serve.

SHARP CHEDDAR

With beta-carotene's orange hue, you won't be able to tell the difference between this cheese and regular cheddar!

■ **MAKES ONE 4-INCH ROUND**

1 cup raw cashews

¼ cup refined coconut oil, plus more for greasing the pan

1 cup raw almonds

1 cup filtered water

¼ cup modified tapioca starch

Beta-carotene from 3 beta-carotene gel caps, squeezed out of the gel caps

1 teaspoon Himalayan salt

2½ tablespoons agar-agar flakes

1 tablespoon apple cider vinegar

EASY PRE-PREP:
Place the cashews in filtered water in a small bowl. Cover and refrigerate overnight.

1. Lightly oil a 4-inch springform pan with coconut oil.

2. Bring 4 cups water to a boil in a medium saucepan over medium-high heat. Add the almonds and blanch them for 1 minute. Drain the almonds in a colander and remove the skins with your fingers (you can compost the skins).

3. Drain the cashews. In the pitcher of a Vitamix, place the cashews, almonds, water, modified tapioca starch, beta-carotene, coconut oil, salt, and agar-agar.

4. Blend on high speed for 1 minute or until smooth.

5. Transfer the mixture to a small saucepan and heat over medium-low heat, **stirring continuously**, until it becomes thick and cheese-like in consistency. (You can use a thermometer and heat the mixture to about 145 degrees F. See page 28 for tips on this technique.)

6. Fold in the vinegar.

7. Pour the cheese into the prepared springform pan. Let it cool, then place it in the fridge overnight to set up.

8. Run a sharp knife around the inside edge of the pan. Release the buckle and remove the ring of the mold. Using the flat edge of a large knife, separate the cheese from the bottom metal round and transfer to a cutting board. With a very sharp knife, slice the cheese and serve.

9. If you want to grate this cheese, turn it out of the mold and place it in a humidifier or wine cooler at 54 degrees F for 1 to 3 weeks. Salt your cheese every few days to prevent black mold from forming.

10. When you feel your cheese is aged sufficiently, cut the round in 8 small wedges, place in plastic wrap, and transfer to the refrigerator for 24 hours. Grate the small cheese wedges on a large grater.

SMOKED GOUDA

Liquid smoke creates gorgeous depths of flavor in this party favorite. ■ **MAKES ONE 4-INCH ROUND**

½ cup raw cashews

½ cup raw almonds

¼ cup refined coconut oil, plus more for greasing

1 cup filtered water

¼ cup modified tapioca starch

1 drop beta-carotene, squeezed out of the gel cap

1 teaspoon Himalayan salt

2½ tablespoons agar-agar flakes

1 teaspoon liquid smoke

EASY PRE-PREP:

Place the cashews in filtered water in a small bowl. Cover and refrigerate overnight. Place the almonds in filtered water in a small bowl. Cover and refrigerate overnight.

1. Lightly oil a 4-inch springform pan with coconut oil.

2. Drain the cashews.

3. Bring 4 cups of water to a boil in a medium saucepan over medium-high heat. Add the almonds and blanch them for 1 minute. Drain the almonds in a colander and remove the skins with your fingers (you can compost the skins).

4. In the pitcher of a Vitamix, place the cashews, almonds, water, the modified tapioca starch, beta-carotene, coconut oil, salt, and agar-agar.

5. Blend on high speed for 1 minute or until smooth.

6. Transfer the mixture to a saucepan and heat over medium-low heat, **stirring continuously**, until it becomes thick and cheese-like in consistency. (You can use a thermometer and heat the mixture to about 145 degrees F. See page 28 for tips on this technique.)

7. Add in the liquid smoke and mix with a rubber spatula to incorporate well.

8. Pour the cheese into the prepared springform pan. Smooth the cheese with the back of a spoon coated with coconut oil. Let the mixture cool, then cover it with a parchment paper round cut to the size of the cheese mold. Transfer the cheese to the fridge overnight to set up.

9. Run a sharp knife around the inside edge of the pan. Release the buckle and remove the ring of the mold. Using the flat edge of a large knife, separate the cheese from the bottom metal round and transfer to a cutting board. With a very sharp knife, slice the cheese and serve.

MOZZARELLA BALLS IN BRINE

Serve this cheese drizzled with the best olive oil and balsamic you can find. In a word: heaven. ■ **MAKES SIX 1-INCH MOZZARELLA BALLS**

1 cup raw cashews

1 cup raw almonds

BRINE

12 cups filtered water

2 tablespoons to ¼ cup Himalayan pink salt

1 cup filtered water

¼ cup modified tapioca starch

¼ cup refined coconut oil

1 teaspoon Himalayan salt

2½ tablespoons agar-agar flakes or 1½ teaspoons agar-agar powder

EASY PRE-PREP:

1. Place the cashews in filtered water in a small bowl. Cover and refrigerate overnight.

2. Rinse the almonds well. Place them in water in a small bowl. Cover and refrigerate overnight.

1. Prepare a brine solution by bringing the water to a boil in a large saucepan over high heat and adding the salt until it dissolves.

2. Transfer the brine to a ceramic bowl and place in the freezer.

3. Bring 4 cups water to a boil in a medium saucepan over medium-high heat. Add the almonds and blanch them for 1 minute. Drain the almonds in a colander and remove the skins with your fingers (you can compost the skins).

4. Drain the cashews. In the bowl of a Vitamix, place the cashews, almonds, water, modified tapioca starch, coconut oil, salt, and agar-agar.

5. Blend on high speed for 1 minute or until smooth.

6. Transfer the mixture to a saucepan and, **stirring continuously,** heat over medium-low heat until it becomes thick and cheese-like in consistency. (You can use a

(recipe continues)

thermometer and heat the mixture to about 145 degrees F. See page 28 for tips on this technique.)

7. Scoop the warm cheese from the saucepan with an ice cream scooper and drop it into the brine.

8. Add 1 cup of ice to the cheese in brine mixture. Cover and transfer to the fridge and refrigerate overnight.

CASHEW-ALMOND MOZZARELLA

I love using coconut milk in this recipe. It creates a fresh, vibrant-tasting cheese. But if you are not a coconut lover, try using homemade almond milk or cashew milk.

■ **MAKES TWO 6 x 3.5 x 2-INCH RECTANGULAR MOLDS**

1 cup raw cashews

1 cup almonds

1 teaspoon apple cider vinegar

1 teaspoon Celtic sea salt

One 15-ounce can coconut milk

¼ cup refined coconut oil

1 cup filtered water

½ cup agar-agar flakes

EASY PRE-PREP:

1. Place the cashews in filtered water in a small bowl. Cover and refrigerate overnight.

2. Rinse the almonds well. Place them in water in a small bowl. Cover and refrigerate overnight.

1. Line two 6-inch rectangular nonstick molds with plastic wrap, leaving enough excess plastic wrap hanging over the sides to wrap the mixture once it's cooled.

2. Bring 4 cups of water to a boil in a medium saucepan over medium-high heat. Add the almonds and blanch them for 1 minute. Drain the almonds in a colander and remove the skins with your fingers (you can compost the skins). Drain the cashews. In the bowl of a food processor, place the almonds and cashews and pulse until they are mealy in texture. Add the vinegar and salt. Pulse again a few times to combine.

3. In a small saucepan over medium heat, combine the coconut milk, coconut oil, and water. When the mixture is warmed through, add the agar-agar flakes and **stir constantly** until the agar-agar is dissolved.

4. With the motor running, pour the mixture into the food processor tube and blend until the mixture is creamy. Stop the

(recipe continues)

motor, remove the lid, and scrape down the sides. Process again to make sure the mixture gets incorporated well. This can also be done in the Vitamix for a smoother texture.

5. Pour the mixture into the prepared molds and let cool on the counter. After the cheese has cooled, cover it with the excess plastic wrap and refrigerate for 24 hours or until firm.

6. Turn the cheese out of the molds and slice.

7. Use as a pizza topping or inside a tomato basil panini!

PROVOLONE

This mild cheese has a smooth, melt-in-your-mouth texture. It's easy to slice and also soft enough to spread. ■ **MAKES ONE 4.5 x 1.5-INCH ROUND**

1 cup raw cashews

1 cup filtered water

¼ cup refined coconut oil, plus more for greasing the pan

¼ cup modified tapioca starch

2 drops beta-carotene, squeezed out of the gel cap

1 teaspoon white truffle oil

1 teaspoon Himalayan salt

1½ teaspoons agar-agar powder or 2½ tablespoons agar-agar flakes

EASY PRE-PREP:
Place the cashews in filtered water in a small bowl. Cover and refrigerate overnight.

1. Lightly oil a 4.5 x 1.5-inch springform pan with coconut oil.

2. Drain the cashews. In the pitcher of a Vitamix, place the cashews, water, modified tapioca starch, beta-carotene, coconut oil, truffle oil, salt, and agar-agar.

3. Blend on high speed for 1 minute or until smooth.

4. Transfer the mixture to a small saucepan over medium-low heat and **stir continuously** until it becomes thick and cheese-like in consistency. (You can use a thermometer and heat the mixture to about 145 degrees F. See page 28 for tips on this technique.)

5. Pour the cheese into the prepared springform pan. Let it cool. Cover with a parchment round cut to the size of the mold, then transfer to the fridge overnight to set up.

6. Turn the cheese out of the mold and place on a serving plate. Using a very sharp knife, slice it and eat it with Kale Chip Crackers (page 189).

EYE OF RA MASCARPONE

A simple, soft, sweet cheese. With love in your heart, mold it into a beautiful work of art. ■ **MAKES 1½ CUPS**

1½ cups cashews

Juice of 2 lemons

EASY PRE-PREP:
Place the cashews in filtered water in a small bowl. Cover and refrigerate overnight.

1. Drain the cashews. In the pitcher of a food processor, place the cashews and lemon juice. Process until the mixture balls up on the side of the bowl.

2. Place the cheese in the center of an 8-inch piece of fine cheesecloth. Gather it into a bundle and tie it with string.

3. Refrigerate the bundle overnight. Return the cheese to the bowl of a food processor and blend until it is fluffy.

4. Shape into a round disc or any shape you desire.

5. Serve with sweet fruit or drizzled with honey.

CASHEW TRUFFLE PARMESAN

Truffle oil brings a nutty, earthy flavor to this classic cheese. ■ **MAKES 2 CUPS**

2 cups raw cashews

1 tablespoon black truffle oil, plus 1 teaspoon for greasing the dish

1 garlic clove

2 tablespoons nutritional yeast

1 teaspoon Celtic sea salt

1 tablespoon chickpea miso paste

1 teaspoon lactic acid or fresh lemon juice

EASY PRE-PREP:
Place the cashews in filtered water in a small bowl. Cover and refrigerate overnight.

1. Lightly oil a 6 x 3 x 2-inch rectangular dish.

2. Drain the cashews. In the bowl of a food processor, place the cashews and pulse until mealy in texture. Add the garlic, nutritional yeast, salt, truffle oil, miso, and lactic acid. Pulse eight times, until the ingredients are well incorporated and you have an aromatic crumble.

3. Press the crumbled parmesan into the prepared dish, making sure you apply consistent, strong pressure to the entire surface until it becomes fused together.

4. Cover the dish and refrigerate overnight.

5. Remove the cheese from the dish by turning it over and hitting the bottom. You may need to use a knife to loosen the edges a bit.

6. Sprinkle over your favorite pasta or salads. Alternatively, shave off thin slices of cheese with a very sharp knife.

7. Serve over an arugula and radicchio salad.

AGED & MULTISTEP CHEESES

AGED CASHEW TRUFFLE CHEESE, 3 WAYS
    Easy Aged Cashew Truffle Cheese
    Cashew–Macadamia Nut Aged Truffle Cheese
    Simple Cashew Truffle Cheese

SUN-DRIED TOMATO MACADAMIA CHEESE

CASHEW BRIE

CASHEW CAMEMBERT

TRIPLE CREAM

MACADAMIA NUT HERBED GOAT CHEESE

AHIMSA GOAT CHEESE

GORGONZOLA, 3 WAYS
    Classic Gorgonzola Blue Cheese
    Gorgonzola Dolce
    Buttery Gorgonzola Dolce

CHIPOTLE CHEDDAR

CASHEW BLEU CHEESE

BURRATA

JAPANESE MISO CHEESE

WHIPPED CASHEW RICOTTA

COCONUT CASHEW CHEESE

SPROUTED ALMOND COCONUT RICOTTA, 2 WAYS

AGED RED PEPPER CASHEW–PINE NUT BLEND

PYRAMID CHEESE

AGED CASHEW TRUFFLE CHEESE, 3 WAYS

Here are three recipes for making delicious Aged Cashew Truffle Cheese. The variations in ingredients and techniques in these recipes show how much creative potential there is in plant-based cheese making! Each of these cheeses has a distinct, nuanced flavor. I'm still discovering new techniques to expand my range, and I hope you will experiment too!

EASY AGED CASHEW TRUFFLE CHEESE

A true *mémoire de* Paris. And it couldn't be simpler to make! ■ **MAKES APPROXIMATELY 2 CUPS**

2 cups raw cashews

1 teaspoon rejuvelac

1 tablespoon fresh shaved truffles

1 teaspoon fresh lemon juice

¼ cup filtered water

½ teaspoon Celtic sea salt

EASY PRE-PREP:
Place the cashews in filtered water in a small bowl. Cover and refrigerate overnight.

1. Drain the cashews. In the pitcher of a Vitamix, place the cashews, rejuvelac, truffles, lemon juice, and water.

2. Blend on medium speed, using the plunger to evenly distribute the mixture until smooth.

3. Place the mixture in the center of an 8-inch piece of fine cheesecloth. Gather it into a bundle and tie it with string.

4. Place the cheesecloth bundle in the dehydrator and dehydrate at 90 degrees F for 24 hours.

5. Open the bundle of cheesecloth and scrape the cheese and rind into the bowl of a food processor. Add the salt.

6. Pulse until the mixture is fluffy. Serve on crackers.

CASHEW–MACADAMIA NUT AGED TRUFFLE CHEESE

This recipe has a similar flavor profile as Easy Aged Cashew Truffle Cheese, but it's fuller and creamier. Use it in Raw Beet Ravioli with Cashew-Macadamia Nut Aged Truffle Cheese (page 121). ■ **MAKES 2 CUPS**

AGED CHEESE BASE

1 cup cashews

1 cup macadamia nuts

¼ cup coconut milk

¼ cup filtered water

½ capsule acidophilus (3-billion-active-culture strain)

CHEESE FLAVORING

1 teaspoon truffle salt, or fresh truffle shavings plus sea salt

¼ teaspoon freshly ground black pepper

1 teaspoon refined coconut oil

EASY PRE-PREP:
Place the cashews in filtered water in a small bowl. Cover and refrigerate overnight.

STEP 1

1. In the pitcher of a Vitamix, place the cashews, macadamia nuts, coconut milk, water and acidophilus. Blend on medium speed, using the plunger to evenly distribute the mixture until well incorporated.

2. Transfer the mixture to the center of an 8-inch piece of fine cheesecloth. Gather the edges and tie them into a bundle with string.

3. Place the cheesecloth bundle in the dehydrator and dehydrate at 90 degrees F for 24 hours.

STEP 2

1. In the bowl of a food processor, place the aged cheese base, truffle salt, pepper, and coconut oil. Use an ice cream scooper to scrape all of your tasty cheese from the cloth. Don't leave any behind.

2. Process until the mixture is well incorporated.

3. Use in Raw Beet Ravioli with Cashew–Macadamia Nut Aged Truffle Cheese (page 121).

SIMPLE CASHEW TRUFFLE CHEESE

Acidophilus gives this cheese a mouthwatering, lightly aged flavor. The key ingredient for this cheese is a great-quality truffle salt—you can find this in any gourmet culinary store. ■ **MAKES 1½ CUPS**

1½ cups raw cashews

1 capsule acidophilus (3-billion-active-culture strain)

2 tablespoons filtered water

1 teaspoon truffle salt

1 teaspoon fresh lemon juice

EASY PRE-PREP:
Place the cashews in filtered water in a small bowl. Cover and refrigerate overnight.

STEP 1

1. Drain the cashews.

2. In the pitcher of a Vitamix, place the cashews, acidophilus, and the water.

3. Blend on medium speed, using the plunger to evenly distribute the mixture until well incorporated. You may have to stop to scrape down the sides as needed.

4. Transfer the mixture to the center of an 8-inch piece of cheesecloth. Gather the edges and tie them into a bundle with string.

5. Place the bundle in the dehydrator at 90 degrees F for 24 hours.

STEP 2

1. Unwrap the cheese and scoop the cheese from the cloth using an ice cream scooper. Place in a medium bowl.

2. Add the truffle salt and lemon juice.

3. Incorporate well, using a small rubber spatula.

4. Adjust the seasonings to taste.

SUN-DRIED TOMATO MACADAMIA CHEESE

Macadamia nuts make a beautifully warm and rich-tasting cheese with the cured flavor of tomatoes and olives. It is a great cheese for an antipasti plate. ■ **MAKES 2 CUPS**

CHEESE BASE

1 cup pine nuts

1 cup macadamia nuts

¼ cup almond milk

½ capsule acidophilus (3-billion-active-culture strain)

CHEESE FLAVORING

2 tablespoons chopped sun-dried tomatoes

1 teaspoon pitted and chopped kalamata olives

1 teaspoon chopped fresh oregano

1 tablespoon chopped fresh basil

3 tablespoons nutritional yeast

½ teaspoon garlic powder

1 teaspoon Celtic sea salt

⅛ teaspoon freshly ground black pepper

½ teaspoon agave

1 teaspoon olive oil

STEP 1

1. In the pitcher of a Vitamix, place the pine nuts, macadamia nuts, almond milk, and acidophilus. Blend on medium speed, using the plunger to evenly distribute the mixture until well incorporated.

2. Using a rubber spatula, transfer the mixture to the center of an 8-inch piece of fine cheesecloth. Gather the edges and tie them into a bundle with string.

3. Place the cheesecloth bundle in the dehydrator and dehydrate at 90 degrees F for 24 hours.

STEP 2

1. In the bowl of a food processor, place the aged cheese base, sun-dried tomatoes, olives, oregano, basil, nutritional yeast, garlic powder, salt, pepper, agave, and olive oil.

2. Pulse until the mixture is well incorporated.

3. Spoon into a rustic, earthy serving dish. Enjoy with warm bread.

NOTE: Chopping the sundried tomatoes, olives, and basil before they go into the food processor prevents overprocessing of the cheese.

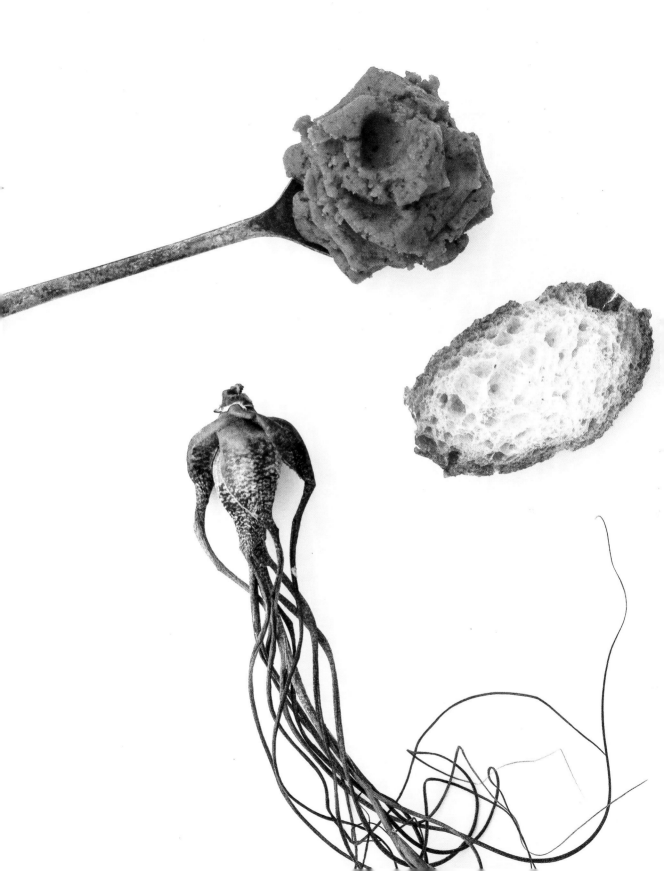

CASHEW BRIE

A delicious expression of the classic. You can enjoy this beauty right after the dehydrator and refrigeration steps. However, the longer you keep it in the humidifier (one to three weeks), the more "Brie-like" it will become. Try it out both ways. I often make a quadruple batch so I can enjoy it right away and have more waiting for me at various stages of aging. ■ **MAKES ONE 4 x 2-INCH ROUND**

2 cups raw cashews

¼ cup unrefined coconut oil, plus more for greasing the pan

¾ cup aquafaba (liquid from canned garbanzo beans)

½ teaspoon Himalayan salt

EASY PRE-PREP:
Place the cashews in filtered water in a small bowl. Cover and refrigerate overnight.

1. Lightly oil a 4-inch pan with coconut oil.

2. Drain the cashews. In the pitcher of a Vitamix, place the cashews, aquafaba, salt, and coconut oil.

3. Process first on medium speed, using the plunger to evenly distribute the mixture.

4. Gradually increase the speed, stopping intermittently to redistribute the mixture until it is smooth.

5. Transfer the mixture to the prepared pan, smooth out the top using a rubber spatula, and cover with a round of parchment paper cut to fit the pan.

6. Dehydrate at 90 degrees F for 24 hours. Transfer to the refrigerator for 24 hours.

7. Run a sharp knife around the edges of the mold. Turn the cheese out onto a cutting board and remove the sides. Using the wide flat side of a large knife, run the flat edge under the metal round, pressing upward to separate the round from the cheese. Smooth the cheese surfaces with a rubber spatula. If desired, place in a humidifier or wine cooler. Rub fine sea salt over your cheese after a few days and then repeat every few days or so to prevent black mold from appearing.

CASHEW CAMEMBERT

This has a fantastic mild taste. The truffle oil gives it the Camembert flavor like its sibling Cashew Brie (page 87), you can eat this immediately after refrigeration, or try your hand at aging. Make a series of rounds by tripling the recipe. Then taste your creations over a three-week period. ■ **MAKES ONE 4 x 2-INCH ROUND**

2 cups raw cashews

2 tablespoons unrefined coconut oil, plus more for greasing the pan

¾ cup aquafaba (liquid from canned garbanzo beans)

½ teaspoon Celtic sea salt

1 teaspoon white truffle oil

EASY PRE-PREP:
Place the cashews in filtered water in a small bowl. Cover and refrigerate overnight.

1. Lightly oil a 4 x 2-inch pan with coconut oil.

2. Drain the cashews. In the pitcher of a Vitamix, place the cashews, aquafaba, salt, coconut oil, and truffle oil.

3. Process first on medium speed, using the plunger to evenly distribute the mixture.

4. Gradually increase the speed, stopping intermittently to redistribute the mixture until it is smooth.

5. Transfer the mixture to the prepared pan and smooth out the top with a rubber spatula. Cover with a round of parchment paper cut to fit the pan.

6. Dehydrate at 90 degrees F for 24 hours. Transfer to the refrigerator for 24 hours.

7. Run a sharp knife around the edges of the mold. Turn the cheese out onto a cutting board and remove the sides. Using the wide flat side of a large knife, run the flat edge under the metal round, pressing upwards to separate the round from the cheese. Smooth the cheese surfaces with rubber spatula If desired, place in a humidifier for 1 to 3 weeks. Rub fine sea salt over your cheese to prevent black mold from appearing.

TRIPLE CREAM

Coconut cream adds decadent body needed to produce this creamy, classic French cheese. Because of the coconut milk, you need to chill this cheese after dehydrating for 48 hours to achieve the best texture. But the level of rich and creamy is well worth the wait!

■ **MAKES APPROXIMATELY 3 CUPS OR TWO 4 x 2-INCH MOLDS**

3 cups cashews

One 15.5-ounce can coconut milk

¼ cup unrefined coconut oil, plus more for greasing the pan

¼ cup aquafaba (liquid from canned garbanzo beans)

1 teaspoon Himalayan salt

1½ teaspoons fresh lemon juice

EASY PRE-PREP:

1. Place the cashews in filtered water in a small bowl. Cover and refrigerate overnight.

2. Place the can of coconut milk in the refrigerator overnight.

---

1. Oil two 4 x 2-inch cheese molds well with coconut oil.

2. Drain the cashews. In the pitcher of a Vitamix, place the cashews, aquafaba, coconut oil, salt, and lemon juice.

3. Scoop out the hardened cream at the top of the coconut milk can and add it to the ingredients in the Vitamix. Reserve the remaining coconut water for a smoothie.

4. Blend on medium speed, using the plunger to evenly distribute the mixture until smooth.

5. Transfer the mixture to the prepared cheese mold. Cover with parchment paper rounds cut to fit the molds.

6. Dehydrate for 24 hours at 90 degrees. Transfer to the refrigerator for 48 hours.

7. Run a sharp knife around the edges of each mold. Turn the cheese out onto a cutting board and remove the sides. Using the wide flat side of a large knife, run the

(recipe continues)

flat edge under the metal round, pressing upward to separate the round from the cheese. Smooth the cheese surfaces with rubber spatula If desired, place in a humidifier for 1 to 3 weeks. Rub fine sea salt over your cheese after a few days and then repeat every few days or so to prevent black mold from appearing. If it does, cut it off and discard. Do not eat it.

MACADAMIA NUT HERBED GOAT CHEESE

A high-vibration version of this pasture favorite that will make you love life. ■ **MAKES TWO 3-INCH LOGS**

2 cups raw macadamia nuts

1 capsule acidophilus (3-billion-active-culture strain)

½ teaspoon plus ⅛ teaspoon Celtic sea salt

½ cup coconut milk

2 teaspoons refined coconut oil

1 teaspoon Himalayan salt

2 tablespoons Greek spices or za'atar (a blend of thyme, oregano, and marjoram)

1. In the pitcher of a Vitamix, place the macadamia nuts, acidophilus, ½ teaspoon Celtic sea salt, coconut milk, coconut oil, and the Himalayan salt. Blend on medium speed, using the plunger to evenly distribute the mixture.

2. Transfer the mixture to the center of an 8-inch piece of cheesecloth. Gather the edges together and tie off your bundle with string. Place the cheese bundle in the dehydrator and dehydrate at 90 degrees F for 24 hours.

3. After the aging is complete, open the cheese bundle and, using an ice cream scooper, remove all the cheese from the cloth and place it (including the rind and center) in the bowl of a food processor. Whip until light and fluffy.

4. Adjust the seasonings to taste. If the taste is too mild, add the remaining ⅛ teaspoon Celtic sea salt.

5. Turn the cheese out onto a work surface and divide it in half. Lay one half in an 8-inch piece of wax paper. Roll the cheese inside the wax paper, moving back and forth to create a log. Repeat with the second half.

6. After the shape is set, even out the ends and gently roll and press in the herbs. Gently wrap the logs in cheesecloth. Transfer to the refrigerator for 2 hours. Serve.

AHIMSA GOAT CHEESE

No goats were harmed in the making of this cheese! Sprouted almonds deliver the perfect texture while apple cider vinegar offers the tang that defines this classic favorite. ■ **MAKES TWO 3-INCH CHEESE LOGS**

2 cups almonds

3½ teaspoons apple cider vinegar, plus more as needed

1 teaspoon Celtic sea salt, plus more as needed

½ cup coconut milk

1 teaspoon refined coconut oil

EASY PRE-PREP:

Soak the almonds for at least 8 hours in filtered water. To sprout them, rinse the almonds with water twice a day for the next 48 hours. You can store them, covered with a piece of cheesecloth, in a cool, dry place. But make sure you drain the water from them completely each time you rinse them. Or, if desired, you can skip the sprouting step and just use soaked almonds. Your cheese will still be delicious.

1. Bring 4 cups of water to a boil in a medium saucepan over medium-high heat. Add the sprouted almonds and quickly blanch them, for 1 minute. Drain the almonds in a colander and remove the skins with your fingers (you can compost the skins).

2. In the pitcher of a Vitamix, place the almonds, vinegar, salt, coconut milk, and coconut oil. Blend on medium speed, using the plunger to evenly distribute the mixture.

3. Transfer the mixture to the center of an 8-inch piece of cheesecloth. Gather the edges and tie them into a bundle with string. Place the cheesecloth bundle in the dehydrator and dehydrate at 90 degrees F for 19 to 24 hours.

4. After the aging is complete, open the cheesecloth bundle and, using an ice cream scooper, scoop the cheese into the bowl of a food processor. Whip until light and fluffy.

5. Adjust the seasonings to taste. If the taste is too mild, add another ⅛ teaspoon vinegar and ⅛ teaspoon salt.

6. Turn the cheese out onto wax paper. Divide the cheese into two equal parts. Roll the cheese inside the wax paper, moving back and forth to create two individual logs.

7. Enjoy with my Beet Goat Cheese Salad (page 127) or with your favorite gluten-free crackers.

GORGONZOLA,
3 WAYS

CLASSIC GORGONZOLA BLUE CHEESE

The superfood power of spirulina in this recipe can only lift you higher, and its marbled blue-green color is gorgeous! ■ **MAKES TWO 4-INCH CHEESE ROUNDS OR ONE 6-INCH ROUND**

4 cups raw cashews

Coconut oil, for greasing the molds

1 capsule acidophilus (3-billion-active-culture strain)

¾ cup coconut milk

1 teaspoon Himalayan salt

¼ to ½ teaspoon spirulina or frozen liquid spirulina

EASY PRE-PREP:
Place the cashews in filtered water in a small bowl. Cover and refrigerate overnight.

1. Lightly oil two 4-inch cheese molds or one 6-inch cheese mold with coconut oil.

2. Drain the cashews. In the bowl of a Vitamix, place the cashews, acidophilus, coconut milk, and salt. Blend on medium speed, using the plunger to evenly distribute the mixture until smooth.

3. Transfer the mixture to a small bowl and sprinkle with the powdered spirulina or break off small chunks of live frozen spirulina and randomly drop them over the cheese mixture. Using a small rubber spatula, marble the spirulina through the mixture to create blue-green veins.

4. Transfer the mixture to the prepared cheese molds and place them in the dehydrator topped with parchment paper rounds cut to fit the tops of the molds.

5. Dehydrate at 90 degrees F for 24 hours.

6. Transfer the molds to the fridge overnight.

7. Remove the cheese from the molds and enjoy, or place the cheese inside a humidifier or wine cooler for 1 to 3 weeks. Rub the outside with fine sea salt every few days to prevent black mold from appearing. The taste of the cheese will continue to develop as it ages.

GORGONZOLA DOLCE

One of my favorite creations, this cheese is absolutely delicious. ■ **MAKES ONE 4-INCH ROUND**

2 cups raw cashews

Coconut oil, for greasing the pan

¼ cup aquafaba (liquid from canned garbanzo beans)

1 teaspoon fresh lemon juice

1 teaspoon Himalayan salt

2 tablespoons nutritional yeast

EASY PRE-PREP:

Place the cashews in filtered water in a small bowl. Cover and refrigerate overnight.

1. Lightly oil a 4-inch mold with coconut oil.

2. Drain the cashews. In the pitcher of a Vitamix, place the cashews, aquafaba, lemon juice, salt, and nutritional yeast. Blend on medium speed, using the plunger to evenly distribute the mixture until well incorporated.

3. Place the cheese inside an 8-inch piece of cheesecloth. Gather the edges and tie off to form a bundle.

4. Place the bundle in the dehydrator and dehydrate at 90 degrees F for 24 hours.

5. Enjoy in my Gorgonzola Dolce Kale Ancient Grain Pasta (page 136).

BUTTERY GORGONZOLA DOLCE

Buttery flavor with a lemony tang even though the recipe is lemon- and butter-free!

■ **MAKES 4½ CUPS**

4 cups raw cashews

Coconut oil, for greasing the pans

1 capsule acidophilus (3-billion-active-culture strain)

¾ cup coconut milk

1 teaspoon Himalayan salt

EASY PRE-PREP:
Place the cashews in filtered water in a small bowl. Cover and refrigerate overnight.

1. Lightly oil two 4-inch springform pans with coconut oil.

2. Drain the cashews. In the pitcher of a Vitamix, place the cashews, acidophilus, coconut milk, and salt. Blend on medium speed, using the plunger to evenly distribute the mixture until smooth.

3. Transfer the mixture to the prepared springform pans. Cover the tops with rounds of parchment paper and place the springform pans in the dehydrator. Dehydrate at 90 degrees F for 24 hours. During dehydration, the cheese will rise as a soufflé does. This is normal.

4. Transfer to the fridge overnight.

5. Remove the cheese from the pans and enjoy.

CHIPOTLE CHEDDAR

This is the perfect cheese filling for your favorite tamales. I adore the melt-in-your-mouth quality of this cheese. It doesn't require aging, Just prep the cashews and Irish moss and you'll be able to whip this cheese up in a just a few minutes so you can get busy wrapping tamales! ■ MAKES 1½ CUPS

1½ cups raw cashews

¼ cup Irish moss

½ cup filtered water

1 teaspoon refined coconut oil

½ teaspoon chipotle chili from a jar, plus 1 tablespoon oil from the jar

½ teaspoon Celtic sea salt, plus more to taste

2 tablespoons nutritional yeast

EASY PRE-PREP:

1. Place the cashews in filtered water in a small bowl. Cover and refrigerate overnight.

2. Rinse the Irish moss very well in a colander until all the sand is removed and the smell of the ocean is gone. Then place it in water in a small bowl. Cover and refrigerate overnight.

1. Drain the Irish moss and place it in the bowl of a Vitamix with the water. Blend on high speed for 1 minute or until it is emulsified. Measure out 2 tablespoons and reserve the rest.

2. Drain the cashews. In a clean pitcher of a Vitamix, place the cashews, the emulsified Irish moss, the coconut oil, chipotle chili, chipotle oil, salt, and nutritional yeast. Blend on medium speed, using the plunger to evenly distribute the ingredients until smooth.

3. Adjust the salt to taste. Spoon the mixture into the center of your tamale before wrapping. Olé!

CASHEW BLEU CHEESE

A work of art, this nut cheese delivers all the pomp and circumstance of provincial "blue." Shhh . . . don't tell anyone, but this cheese gets its color from the superfood spirulina. It's packed with flavors that are fresh and healthy and it still has a full creamy texture. "But does it really taste exactly like blue cheese," you ask? Thankfully, no! It tastes much better! ■ **MAKES ONE 4-INCH MOLD**

2 cups raw cashews

¼ cup Irish moss

½ cup filtered water

1 tablespoon nutritional yeast

1½ teaspoons Celtic sea salt

2 teaspoons refined coconut oil

¼ teaspoon garlic powder

1 capsule acidophilus
  (3-billion-active-culture strain)

¼ cup aquafaba (water from a
  15.5-ounce can of garbanzo beans)

½ teaspoon powdered spirulina
  or frozen live spirulina

EASY PRE-PREP:

1. Place the cashews in filtered water in a small pitcher. Cover and refrigerate overnight.

2. Rinse the Irish moss very well in a colander until all of the sand is removed and the smell of the ocean is gone. Then place it in filtered water in a small bowl. Cover and refrigerate overnight.

---

1. Drain the Irish moss and place it in the bowl of a Vitamix along with the water. Blend on high speed for 1 minute or until it is emulsified. Measure out 2 tablespoons and reserve the rest.

2. Drain the cashews. In a clean pitcher of the Vitamix, place the cashews, emulsified Irish moss, the nutritional yeast, salt, coconut oil, garlic powder, acidophilus, and aquafaba.

3. Blend on medium speed, using the plunger to evenly distribute the mixture. Transfer the mixture to a cheese mold.

4. Sprinkle the spirulina over the cheese and, using a small spatula, marble it through in all directions. Do not overmix or your cheese will turn green.

5. Place the cheese mold in the dehydrator and dehydrate at 90 degrees F for 24 hours. Refrigerate overnight.

6. Serve, or store in a humidifier or wine cooler for up to 3 weeks.

BURRATA

Sprouted, blanched almonds create a clean, fresh cheese—a simple treasure of soft and creamy cheese that is a delight to discover.

■ **MAKES APPROXIMATELY 2 CUPS**

2 cups raw almonds

1 tablespoon apple cider vinegar

1 teaspoon Himalayan salt

½ cup coconut milk plus 1 cup for soaking

1 teaspoon coconut oil

EASY PRE-PREP:

Soak the almonds for at least 8 hours in filtered water. To sprout them, rinse the almonds with filtered water twice a day for the next 48 hours. You can store them, covered with a piece of cheesecloth, in a cool, dry place. But make sure you drain the water from them completely each time you rinse them. Or if desired you can skip the sprouting step and just use soaked almonds. Your cheese will still be delicious.

1. Bring 4 cups of water to a boil in a medium saucepan over medium-high heat. Add the almonds and quickly blanch them, for 1 minute. Drain the almonds in a colander and remove the skins with your fingers (you can compost them).

2. In the pitcher of a Vitamix, place the almonds, vinegar, salt, ½ cup coconut milk, and the coconut oil. Blend on medium speed, using the plunger to evenly distribute the mixture until well incorporated and smooth.

3. Transfer the ingredients to the center of an 8-inch piece of fine cheesecloth. Gather the edges and tie them into a bundle with string. Hang the cheese bundle on a hook on the wall or on the underside of a cabinet. Place a small dish beneath it to catch the liquid. Hang overnight or until a soft darkened rind forms.

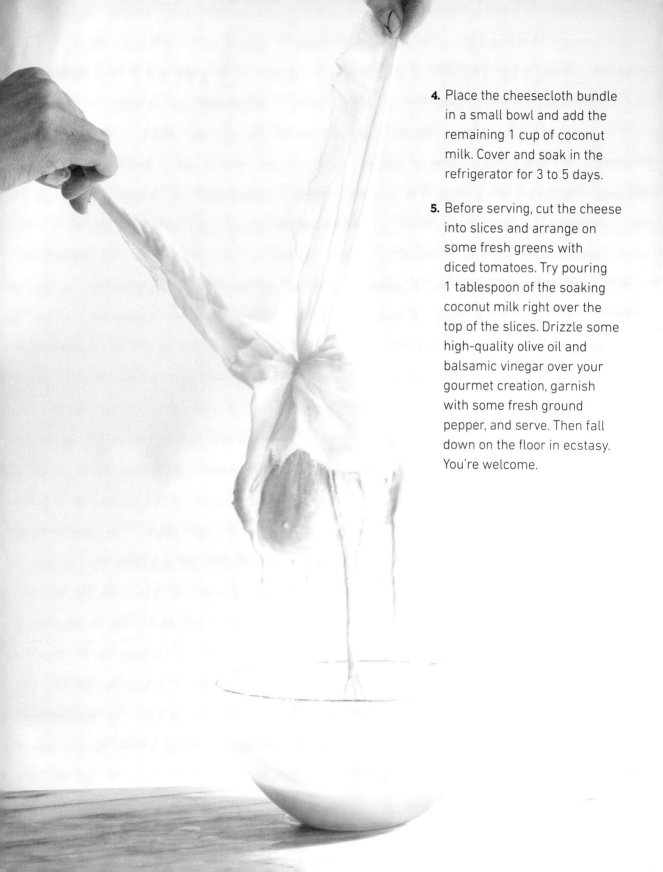

4. Place the cheesecloth bundle in a small bowl and add the remaining 1 cup of coconut milk. Cover and soak in the refrigerator for 3 to 5 days.

5. Before serving, cut the cheese into slices and arrange on some fresh greens with diced tomatoes. Try pouring 1 tablespoon of the soaking coconut milk right over the top of the slices. Drizzle some high-quality olive oil and balsamic vinegar over your gourmet creation, garnish with some fresh ground pepper, and serve. Then fall down on the floor in ecstasy. You're welcome.

JAPANESE MISO CHEESE

Fermented garlic adds sweet, mild notes to this Asian fusion cheese. Spread onto Buckwheat Crackers (page 190) and top with dried seaweed for a delicious appetizer. (See photo pages 78-79.)

■ MAKES 2 CUPS CHEESE SPREAD OR ONE 4-INCH CHEESE ROUND

1 cup raw cashews

1 cup fresh coconut meat from a brown coconut (do not substitute with coconut flakes)

2/3 cup aquafaba (liquid from canned garbanzo beans)

1 tablespoon coconut oil, plus more for greasing the cheese molds

2 fermented black garlic cloves

1/2 tablespoon chickpea miso paste

1 tablespoon nutritional yeast

1/2 teaspoon apple cider vinegar

1 small seaweed sprig, any variety

Pinch of large-grain Celtic sea salt

EASY PRE-PREP:

1. Place the cashews in filtered water in a small bowl. Cover and refrigerate overnight.

2. In the bowl of a food processor pulse the fresh coconut pieces until mealy in texture. Cover and refrigerate until ready to use.

1. Lightly oil one 4-inch round cheese mold with coconut oil.

2. Drain the cashews. In the pitcher of a Vitamix, place the cashews, coconut, aquafaba, and coconut oil. Blend on medium speed, using the plunger to evenly distribute the mixture until well incorporated and smooth. You may have to stop and scrape down the sides with a rubber spatula and then start again.

3. Transfer the cheese to the prepared cheese mold. Place the cheese mold in the dehydrator and dehydrate at 90 degrees F for 24 hours.

4. Remove the cheese from the mold and place in the bowl of a food processor. Add the garlic, miso, nutritional yeast, and vinegar. Process for 1 minute or until smooth. Transfer the mixture to a small decorative serving dish. Alternatively, transfer it into the prepared mold and refrigerate for 24 hours.

WHIPPED CASHEW RICOTTA

A fluffy ricotta perfect for everything Italian and a delicious filling for my Raw Manicotti with Whipped Cashew Ricotta (page 131). ■ **MAKES 2 CUPS**

2 cups raw cashews

¼ cup Irish moss

¾ cup filtered water

1 teaspoon rejuvelac

2 teaspoons fresh lemon juice

2 tablespoons aquafaba

¼ teaspoon Celtic sea salt

EASY PRE-PREP:

1. Place the cashews in filtered water in a small bowl. Cover and refrigerate overnight.

2. Rinse the Irish moss very well in a colander until all of the sand is removed and the smell of the ocean is gone. Then place it in water in a small bowl. Cover and refrigerate overnight.

1. Drain the Irish moss and place it in the pitcher of a Vitamix with ½ cup water. Blend on high speed for 1 minute or until it is emulsified. Measure out 2 tablespoons and reserve the rest.

2. In a clean bowl of the Vitamix, place the cashews, emulsified Irish moss, rejuvelac, remaining ¼ cup water, and salt. Blend on medium speed, using the plunger to evenly distribute the mixture, stopping and starting until everything is well incorporated.

3. Transfer the cheese to the center of an 8-inch piece of fine cheesecloth. Gather the edges and tie them into a bundle with string.

4. Place the cheesecloth bundle in the dehydrator and dehydrate at 90 degrees F for 24 hours.

5. Transfer the cheese to the bowl of a food processor and pulse until the texture is light and fluffy.

COCONUT CASHEW CHEESE

This tropical combination makes for a versatile cheese base. You can create a whiter hue by adding more coconut than cashew. ▪ **MAKES TWO 4-INCH ROUNDS**

2 cups raw cashews

2 tablespoons coconut oil, plus more for greasing the cheese molds

2 cups fresh coconut meat from a brown coconut (do not substitute with coconut flakes)

¾ cup aquafaba (liquid from canned garbanzo beans)

1 teaspoon Himalayan salt

Edible flower petals, for garnish

EASY PRE-PREP:
Place the cashews in filtered water in a small bowl. Cover and refrigerate overnight.

1. Lightly oil two 4-inch cheese molds with coconut oil.

2. In the bowl of a food processor, place the coconut and pulse until mealy in texture. Set aside.

3. Drain the cashews. In the pitcher of a Vitamix place the cashews, coconut, aquafaba, salt, and coconut oil. Blend on medium speed, using the plunger to evenly distribute the mixture until smooth. You may need to stop the blender and scrape down the sides using a rubber spatula a few times.

4. Transfer the mixture to the prepared cheese molds. Cover the molds with parchment paper rounds cut to fit the molds.

5. Place the cheese molds in the dehydrator and dehydrate at 90 degrees F for 24 hours. Refrigerate overnight.

6. Remove the cheese from the molds. Arrange on plates and decorate with edible flower petals.

SPROUTED ALMOND COCONUT RICOTTA, 2 WAYS

Creamy, airy textures of deliciousness to add to your lasagnas, pastas, and Italian desserts. Fresh coconut makes for a fresh taste. You can find large fresh chunks of coconut already removed from the shell at any health market. *Bellissima!* ■ **MAKES THREE 4-INCH ROUNDS**

2 cups raw almonds

3 tablespoons refined coconut oil, plus more for greasing the cheese molds or springform pans

2 cups fresh coconut meat from a brown coconut (do not substitute with coconut flakes)

One 15-ounce can coconut milk

1 teaspoon Himalayan salt

1 capsule acidophilus (3-billion-active-culture strain)

NOTE: As the coconut ages, you may see some pink veins, which is pretty!

EASY PRE-PREP:

1. Soak the almonds for at least 8 hours in filtered water. To sprout them, rinse the almonds with water twice a day for the next 48 hours. You can store them, covered with a piece of cheesecloth, in a cool, dry place. But make sure you drain the water from them completely each time you rinse them. Or, if desired, you can skip the sprouting step and just use soaked almonds. Your cheese will still be delicious.

2. In a food processor, pulse the chunks of coconut meat until mealy in texture. Store covered in the fridge until ready to use.

1. Bring 4 cups water to a boil in a medium saucepan over medium-high heat. Add the almonds and blanch them for 1 minute. Drain the almonds in a colander and remove the skins with your fingers (you can compost the skins).

2. Lightly oil three 4-inch cheese molds or springform pans.

3. In the pitcher of a Vitamix, place the almonds, coconut meat, coconut milk, salt, coconut oil, and acidophilus. Blend on high speed, using the plunger to evenly distribute the mixture until well incorporated and very smooth.

4. Pour the cheese into the three prepared cheese molds, gently shaking the molds to

redistribute the mixture evenly. Smooth out the tops with a rubber spatula.

5. Cover the tops with rounds of parchment paper cut to fit the molds. Place the cheese molds in the dehydrator and dehydrate at 90 degrees F for 24 hours. Now, the cheese is ready to add into your lasagna and Italian desserts.

6. Turn the cheese out of the mold onto a tray or serving dish. Using the flat side of a large knife, run the edge of the knife between the cheese and the round to remove the metal round.

7. Alternatively, if you don't plan to use the cheese in another dish, continue aging it for another 24 hours, for a total of 48 hours.

8. After the dehydration is complete, transfer the mold to the refrigerator for another 24 hours. This produces a firmer cheese. Serve with flax crackers, fruit, or dessert.

AGED RED PEPPER CASHEW–PINE NUT BLEND

Combining two varieties of nuts produces a slightly different texture that is smooth and delicious. The red pepper flakes kick the flavor up a notch. ■ **MAKES ONE 4-INCH ROUND**

1 cup cashews

1 teaspoon refined coconut oil, plus more for greasing the cheese mold

1 cup pine nuts

¼ cup filtered water

½ capsule acidophilus (3-billion-active-culture strain)

1 tablespoon nutritional yeast

1 teaspoon garlic powder

½ teaspoon mild chili pepper

1 teaspoon Himalayan salt

One 1.59 ounce jar red pepper flakes

Fresh oregano leaves, for garnish

EASY PRE-PREP:
Place the cashews in filtered water in a small bowl. Cover and refrigerate overnight.

1. Lightly oil a 4-inch cheese mold with coconut oil.

2. Drain the cashews. In the pitcher of a Vitamix, place the cashews, pine nuts, water, the acidophilus, coconut oil, nutritional yeast, garlic powder, chili, and salt.

3. Blend on medium speed, using the plunger to evenly distribute the mixture until well incorporated. You may need to stop the blender a few times to scrape down the sides of the bowl.

4. Transfer the cheese to the prepared cheese mold. Smooth out the top using a rubber spatula. Top with a round of parchment paper.

5. Place the cheese mold in the dehydrator and dehydrate at 90 degrees F for 24 hours. Transfer to the refrigerator overnight.

6. Remove the cheese from the mold and press the red pepper flakes onto the outside. Garnish with fresh oregano.

PYRAMID CHEESE

Bold spices make this cheese an artful creation reminiscent of an exotic journey to a Mayan temple. ■ MAKES 2 CUPS

CHEESE BASE

1 cup cashews

1 cup pine nuts

½ capsule acidophilus (3-billion-active-culture strain)

CHEESE FLAVORING

¼ cup nutritional yeast

1 garlic clove, minced

¼ teaspoon garlic powder

1 teaspoon ground cumin, plus extra for garnish

1 tablespoon fresh oregano

½ teaspoon freshly ground black pepper

2 teaspoons almond milk

1 teaspoon coconut oil

¾ teaspoon Himalayan salt

¾ teaspoon agave or ½ date, pitted

Ground cumin and fresh herbs, for dusting

EASY PRE-PREP:
Place the cashews in filtered water in a small bowl. Cover and refrigerate overnight.

STEP 1

1. Drain the cashews. In the pitcher of a Vitamix, place the cashews, pine nuts, ¼ cup water, and the acidophilus. Blend on medium speed, using the plunger to evenly distribute the mixture until well incorporated.

2. Transfer the mixture to the center of an 8-inch piece of fine cheesecloth. Gather the edges and tie them into a bundle with string.

3. Place the cheesecloth bundle in the dehydrator and dehydrate at 90 degrees F for 24 hours.

STEP 2

1. In the bowl of a food processor, place the aged cheese base, nutritional yeast, garlic, garlic powder, cumin, oregano, pepper, almond milk, coconut oil, salt, and agave.

2. Process until the mixture is well incorporated.

3. Shape the mixture into a pyramid with a 3-inch base.

4. Turn a deep bowl upside down and place the pyramid on top of the inverted bowl.

5. Dust with cumin and some fresh herbs.

DISHES

RAW BEET RAVIOLI WITH CASHEW–
MACADAMIA NUT AGED TRUFFLE CHEESE

PROVOLONE BAKED IN PHYLLO DOUGH

STUFFED RED POTATO BITES

BEET GOAT CHEESE SALAD

GREEK SALAD STACK

RAW MANICOTTI WITH WHIPPED
CASHEW RICOTTA

SMOKY BUTTERNUT CHEDDAR SAUCE
WITH BLACKENED BROCCOLI

MAC AND CHEESE WITH GARLIC SPINACH

GORGONZOLA DOLCE KALE ANCIENT GRAIN PASTA

SPAGHETTI SQUASH WITH 3-HERB
MACADAMIA–PINE NUT CHEESY PESTO

LASAGNA WITH GARDEN TOMATO SAUCE

BLACKENED CAULIFLOWER WITH
CLASSIC CASHEW CHEESE SAUCE

ALMOND FETTUCCINE ALFREDO

LEMON CASHEW MUNG BEAN FETTUCCINE

N'EGGS BENNIE WITH HOLLANDAISE SAUCE
AND COCONUT BACON

RAW BEET RAVIOLI WITH CASHEW–MACADAMIA NUT AGED TRUFFLE CHEESE

Arguably the best appetizer ever invented. This dish was featured in the *New York Times* piece "Vegans Go Glam" by Jeff Gordinier featuring my husband, Rich Roll, and me. These fabulous hors d'oeuvres stole the show!

You'll need a mandoline and a beautiful plate for serving. ■ **SERVES 6**

2 medium raw beets or 2 medium watermelon radishes

1 tablespoon great-quality olive oil

Pinch of Celtic sea salt

Cashew–Macadamia Nut Aged Truffle Cheese (page 82)

Fresh mint or basil, for garnish

1. Using a mandoline, and wearing a protective glove, slice the beets or radishes into paper-thin slices. You may have to test a few to get just the right thickness.

2. In a small bowl, combine the beets, olive oil, and salt. Toss to coat.

3. Set aside for 20 minutes.

4. On a clean surface, make a layer of paper towels. Arrange the beet rounds in rows, turning them over once to blot any excess oil.

5. Using a butter knife, spread 1½ teaspoons of the truffle cheese on the centers of the rounds. Top with another beet round or, alternatively, serve them open-faced.

6. Garnish each with a mint leaf. Serve on a cutting board or on a beautiful serving plate.

PROVOLONE BAKED IN PHYLLO DOUGH

This provolone has a creamy, soft, and warm texture when it's baked inside a flaky crust. You could also try this recipe with Cashew Cheddar (page 61). ■ **MAKES ONE 4-INCH ROUND**

1 cup raw cashews

¼ cup refined coconut oil

1 cup filtered water

1 teaspoon pink salt

¼ cup modified tapioca starch

2 drops beta-carotene squeezed out of the gel cap

1 teaspoon white truffle oil

1½ teaspoons agar-agar powder or 2½ tablespoons agar-agar flakes

6 vegan phyllo dough sheets

1 tablespoon Earth Balance vegan butter, melted, or 1 teaspoon melted coconut oil

EASY PRE-PREP

Place the raw cashews in filtered water in a small bowl. Cover and refrigerate overnight.

1. Lightly oil a 4-inch mold with coconut oil.

2. Drain the cashews. In the pitcher of a Vitamix, add the cashews, water, tapioca, beta-carotene, coconut oil, white truffle oil and agar-agar. Blend on high until smooth or for 1 full minute.

3. Transfer to a saucepan and heat on medium-low heat, **stirring continuously** until it becomes thick and cheeselike in consistency. It will start to pull away clean from the sides of the pan when ready. (You can use a thermometer and heat it to about 145 degrees. See pg. 28 for tips on technique.)

4. Pour the cheese into the prepared mold. Let it cool, cover with a parchment round cut to the size of the mold, then transfer to the fridge overnight to set up.

5. Follow package directions for thawing and preparing the phyllo dough sheets. Lay six sheets in a stack. Remove the cheese from the mold and turn out into the center of the phyllo dough. Wrap the cheese with individual layers of the phyllo, carefully sealing the edges with vegan butter. Bake at 400 degrees for about 15 minutes or until it turns golden brown.

STUFFED RED POTATO BITES

A twist on the classic baked potato with sour cream, these petite hearty bites deliver a creamy smoky treat. ■ **SERVES 6**

6 egg-size red potatoes, scrubbed

Celtic sea salt and freshly ground black pepper

Classic Sour Cream (page 185)

¼ cup smoked tea, seaweed, or Coconut Bacon (page 148), for garnish

Dry sprigs of Irish moss, for garnish

1. In a medium pan over medium-high heat, bring 8 cups of water to a boil and add the potatoes.

2. Cook the potatoes until they are tender when pierced with a fork, then drain them in a colander.

3. Cut off the top third of each potato and discard (you can compost the tops).

4. Using a mini scooper or small spoon, create a well inside the potato.

5. Place the potatoes in small spice bowls or cut off the bottoms of each potato to give you a flat edge to place on a tray.

6. Sprinkle the potatoes well with a pinch of sea salt and pepper.

7. Fill the wells with sour cream.

8. Garnish with smoked tea, seaweed, or Coconut Bacon, and sprigs of Irish moss.

NOTE: Smoked tea is a specialty tea that has been infused with a smoky flavor. It can be used in soups or eaten as a garnish.

BEET GOAT CHEESE SALAD

Creamy, tangy goat cheese and sweet beet roots are the perfect combination for a lively salad. ■ **SERVES 4**

2 tablespoons vegan butter

1 cup raw walnuts

4 tablespoons organic coconut sugar

2 small red beets

1 head of butter lettuce

6 tablespoons Macadamia Nut Herbed Goat Cheese (page 95)

DRESSING

1 tablespoon sherry vinegar

1 teaspoon Celtic sea salt

2 tablespoons olive oil

Juice of 1 lemon

Freshly ground black pepper

1. In a medium saucepan over low heat, melt the vegan butter. Add the walnuts and coconut sugar and stir to coat until the sugar crystallizes on the walnuts. Set aside.

2. Wash the beets. Cut off the stem and root and discard (or you can compost them). Place the beets in a small saucepan over high heat, cover with water, and boil for 30 minutes or until tender.

3. Drain the beets in a colander. With the water running, rub the skins off the beets using your fingers. Dice the beets into small cubes. Set aside.

4. In the bottom of a medium salad bowl, add the vinegar, salt, olive oil, lemon juice, and pepper. Whisk together until combined.

5. Wash any dirt from the lettuce leaves and dry on paper towels. Tear the lettuce into bite-size pieces and place them on top of the dressing. Toss to coat.

6. Transfer the lettuce to four serving plates. Arrange some beet cubes along with pieces of herbed goat cheese on each plate. Garnish with the caramelized walnuts.

GREEK SALAD STACK

Tofu feta magically infuses this salad with bold notes of Greece. ■ SERVES 6

DRESSING

¼ cup extra-virgin olive oil

1 teaspoon apple cider vinegar

1 tablespoon fresh lemon juice

1 teaspoon Celtic sea salt

Freshly ground black pepper

SALAD

1 head romaine lettuce

2 roma tomatoes

1 large cucumber

2 cups kalamata olives, pitted

Feta Tofu Cheese (page 181)

Freshly ground black pepper

1 bunch fresh Italian oregano, for garnish

FOR THE DRESSING:

1. In a large salad bowl, whisk together the olive oil, vinegar, lemon juice, salt, and pepper.

FOR THE SALAD:

1. Wash romaine lettuce leaves and dry with a towel. Slice the tomatoes and cucumbers into rounds. Halve the kalamata olives.

2. On a cutting board, arrange an entire leaf the length of the board and spread with a thick layer of feta cheese. Repeat with the remaining lettuce and feta. Add the tomatoes, cucumber, and olives.

3. Drizzle with the dressing. Garnish with fresh-cracked pepper and parsley.

RAW MANICOTTI WITH WHIPPED CASHEW RICOTTA

Easy, fresh, and flavorful. You'll need a mandoline and a beautiful Italian ceramic plate to serve it on. ■ **SERVES 6**

4 medium zucchini

1 tablespoon olive oil

Pinch of Celtic sea salt

Whipped Cashew Ricotta (page 109)

Rosemary sprigs, for garnish

1. Cut off and discard the ends of the zucchini, leaving a straight edge on each end. Using protective gloves, slice the zucchini lengthwise into paper-thin ribbons on a mandoline.

2. In a medium bowl, toss the zucchini ribbons in the olive oil and salt. Set aside for 20 minutes.

3. Arrange a layer of paper towels on a clean surface. Lay out the zucchini ribbons and turn them once to let any excess oil drain onto the paper towels.

4. Place a zucchini ribbon flat on a serving plate and spoon 2 teaspoons of cashew ricotta onto one end.

5. Carefully roll up the cheese-filled zucchini ribbon to make your manicotti.

6. Repeat with the rest of the zucchini ribbons, then arrange them on a serving plate and garnish with a rosemary sprig.

SMOKY BUTTERNUT CHEDDAR SAUCE WITH BLACKENED BROCCOLI

Who can resist a cheesy sauce to pour over greens? This one is full of flavor without the heaviness of dairy cheese. The blackened broccoli gives the dish a hint of barbecue flavor. ■ SERVES 4

¼ cup raw cashews

1 butternut squash

½ teaspoon garlic powder

1 teaspoon Celtic sea salt

2 tablespoons nutritional yeast

1 tablespoon coconut oil

1 teaspoon liquid smoke

1 head broccoli, cut into florets

½ cup filtered water

Freshly ground black pepper

¼ cup Coconut Bacon, for garnish (page 148)

NOTE: The consistency of the sauce is determined by the water content in the squash. If you want a thicker sauce, add another ¼ cup cashews. Or for a nut-free version, add 1 tablespoon vegan butter.

EASY PRE-PREP:
Place the cashews in filtered water in a small bowl. Cover and refrigerate overnight.

1. Preheat the oven to 350 degrees F.

2. Place the entire butternut squash on a wire rack and bake for about 40 minutes, until the skin is browned and the squash is soft to the touch. Remove the squash from the oven and place it on a cutting board. Slice it open and remove the seeds. Measure out 1 cup squash for this recipe (you can use the remainder for a soup).

3. Drain the cashews. In the pitcher of a Vitamix or high-powered blender, place the squash, cashews, garlic powder, salt, nutritional yeast, 2 teaspoons of the coconut oil, and liquid smoke. Process for 1 minute.

4. In a cast-iron skillet over high heat, blacken the broccoli in the remaining 1 teaspoon coconut oil. When the broccoli has sufficient charring, remove the skillet from the heat, add the water, and cover the skillet with a tight-fitting lid to allow the broccoli to steam.

5. Arrange the broccoli on a beautiful serving platter and pour the cheddar sauce over the broccoli.

6. Season with pepper and garnish with Coconut Bacon.

MAC AND CHEESE WITH GARLIC SPINACH

Garlic spinach brings life to this comfort food staple. ■ **SERVES 4**

1 cup raw cashews

2 cups fresh spinach

1 tablespoon olive oil

½ shallot, sliced

1 garlic clove, minced

¼ cup chickpea miso paste

1 tablespoon fresh lemon juice

1 teaspoon Celtic sea salt, plus more to taste

½ teaspoon garlic powder

¼ teaspoon freshly ground black pepper, plus more for a garnish

1 tablespoon nutritional yeast

1 cup boiling water

1 package gluten-free pasta

EASY PRE-PREP:

Place the cashews in filtered water in a small bowl. Cover and refrigerate overnight.

1. Wash the spinach in a salad spinner.

2. In a cast-iron skillet over medium heat, heat the olive oil. Add the shallot and sauté until browned. Add the garlic and stir with a wooden spoon. Add the spinach and sauté until it is wilted and infused with the garlic and onion.

3. Drain the cashews. In the pitcher of a Vitamix, place the cashews, miso, lemon juice, salt, garlic powder, pepper, nutritional yeast, and boiling water.

4. Blend on medium speed for 2 minutes or until thickened and creamy. Adjust the seasonings to taste.

5. Bring a large pot of water to a boil over medium-high heat and cook the pasta according to the package directions. Drain the pasta in a colander and rinse with hot water.

6. Transfer the pasta to a large serving dish. Pour the cashew cheese sauce over the pasta and mix thoroughly with a wooden spoon.

7. Arrange the spinach in a mound on top.

8. Season with pepper and a pinch of salt.

GORGONZOLA DOLCE KALE ANCIENT GRAIN PASTA

Gorgonzola dolce delivers a full-bodied, creamy taste that perfectly offsets the astringent quality of kale in this hearty pasta dish. ■ **SERVES 6**

One 16-ounce package gourmet (ancient grain) pasta

1 teaspoon olive oil

Pinch of Celtic sea salt, plus more for garnish

1 cup baby kale

1½ cups Gorgonzola Dolce (page 100)

Freshly cracked black pepper

1. Bring a medium pot of water to a boil over medium-high heat and cook the pasta according to the package directions.

2. In a small bowl, place the olive oil and salt. Add the kale and massage the oil into the leaves to tenderize them.

3. Drain the pasta in a colander and rinse with hot water.

4. In a medium bowl, add ¾ cup of the Gorgonzola Dolce and place the warm pasta on top. Using tongs, toss the pasta until it is well coated with the cheese.

5. Using tongs, arrange the pasta in the middle of the plate, making circular motions to form a mound.

6. Add individual leaves of the tenderized kale and garnish with small pieces of the remaining ¾ cup of gorgonzola.

7. Season with pepper and a pinch of salt.

SPAGHETTI SQUASH WITH 3-HERB MACADAMIA–PINE NUT CHEESY PESTO

Using spaghetti squash as a stand-in for pasta is a fantastically healthy way to enjoy the full experience of this vibrant, tasty pesto. ■ **SERVES 6**

1 whole spaghetti squash

1 tablespoon walnut oil

3-Herb Macadamia–Pine Nut Cheesy Pesto (page 50)

1 teaspoon Celtic sea salt

Flax crackers, for garnish

1. Preheat the oven to 350 degrees F.

2. Place the entire spaghetti squash in the oven on a wire rack. Bake for 45 minutes or until soft.

3. On a cutting board, cut the squash in half and remove the seeds. Using a spoon, scrape out the insides and place in a medium bowl. The squash will resemble pasta-like strands.

4. Drizzle the walnut oil over the pasta and sprinkle with salt.

5. Add the pesto to the spaghetti squash, reserving a few tablespoons for garnish. Toss with tongs until the spaghetti squash is well coated.

6. Divide among six plates, garnish with pesto crumble, and top each with a flax cracker.

LASAGNA WITH GARDEN TOMATO SAUCE

Using potatoes as noodles is a lovely gluten-free variation on lasagna. The secret ingredient to this delicious dish is Whipped Cashew Ricotta (page 109). Note: Wear a protective glove when using a mandoline. ■ **SERVES 6**

LASAGNA

10 medium golden potatoes, skins on

3 tablespoons olive oil

3 teaspoons Celtic sea salt

2 garlic cloves, minced

2 bunches fresh spinach

Whipped Cashew Ricotta (page 109)

2 medium shallots, peeled and sliced

Freshly cracked black pepper

RAW TOMATO SAUCE

6 sun-dried tomatoes

1 cup cherry tomatoes

3 kalamata olives, pitted

1 tablespoon fresh oregano

1 tablespoon fresh basil

½ teaspoon balsamic vinegar

Juice of 1 small lemon

FOR THE LASAGNA

1. Using a mandoline or a food processor fitted with the slicing attachment, slice the potatoes into very thin, transparent slices.

2. In a medium bowl, toss the potatoes with tablespoons olive oil and 1 teaspoon salt.

3. In a cast-iron skillet over medium heat, sauté the garlic in 1 tablespoon of olive oil. Add the spinach and sauté until the garlic is infused in the spinach. Do not overcook.

4. Arrange a layer of potatoes in the bottom of a 9 x 13-inch baking dish. Then add another layer, crosswise, on top of the first layer to form a basketweave pattern. Place tablespoon-sized dollops of both spinach and ricotta, keeping them spaced about 2 inches apart. Garnish with shallot slices and pepper and sprinkle with a pinch of salt. Repeat, adding layers until the baking dish is filled.

FOR THE GARDEN TOMATO SAUCE

1. Soak the sun-dried tomatoes in very hot water for 30 minutes or until soft. Drain.

2. In the pitcher of a Vitamix, place the cherry tomatoes, sun-dried tomatoes, olives, oregano, basil, balsamic vinegar, and lemon juice. Blend on medium speed for 1 minute or until smooth.

3. Preheat the oven to 350 degrees F. Pour the tomato sauce over the top of the lasagna and bake for 45 minutes or until the potatoes are tender.

BLACKENED CAULIFLOWER WITH CLASSIC CASHEW CHEESE SAUCE

This recipe is inspired by Miznon, an amazing Parisian café. One of their specialties is blackened cauliflower. When I tried it at home, I found the perfect pairing for my warm cashew cheese. ■ **SERVES 6**

1 head cauliflower

2 tablespoons refined coconut oil

1 teaspoon Celtic sea salt

Freshly ground black pepper

Classic Cashew Cheese Sauce
  (page 54)

1. Preheat the oven to broil.

2. Place the cauliflower head on a rimmed baking dish and brush generously with the coconut oil.

3. Sprinkle with salt and pepper.

4. Broil for about 20 minutes, watching it carefully so that it becomes blackened. Turn the oven off and leave the cauliflower inside with the door closed for another 20 minutes.

5. Transfer the cauliflower head to a serving plate and pour the Cashew Cheese Sauce over the top. Serve!

ALMOND FETTUCCINE ALFREDO

A creamy sauce for your favorite classic pasta! Now you can truly enjoy this classic recipe minus the stomachache and heavy feeling. It's a joy to enjoy! ■ MAKES 2 CUPS

2 cups raw almonds, plus more for garnish

2 tablespoons chickpea miso paste

1 tablespoon white truffle oil

1 tablespoon refined coconut oil

2 tablespoons nutritional yeast

½ teaspoon Celtic sea salt

1 cup boiling water

One 16-ounce package gluten-free fettuccine

Freshly ground black pepper

Fresh herbs

EASY PRE-PREP:
Place the almonds in filtered water in a small bowl. Cover and refrigerate overnight.

1. Bring 4 cups water to boil in a medium saucepan over medium-high heat. Add the almonds and blanch them for 1 minute. Drain the almonds in a colander and remove the skins with your fingers (you can compost the skins).

2. In the pitcher of a Vitamix, place the almonds, miso, truffle oil, coconut oil, nutritional yeast, salt, and water.

3. Blend on medium speed, using the plunger to evenly distribute the mixture until smooth.

4. Add more hot water in increments of ¼ cup to reach the desired consistency. Adjust the seasonings to taste. If you add more water, you can have a lighter sauce.

5. Bring a medium pot of water to a boil over medium-high heat and cook the fettuccine according to the package directions. Drain the fettuccine in a colander and rinse with hot water.

6. Pour the sauce over the fettuccine. Garnish with pepper and herbs.

LEMON CASHEW MUNG BEAN FETTUCINE

This lemony-flavored cheese is great mixed with bean pastas. There are some amazing bean pastas in the market today. I love this combination and my kids do too! ■ **SERVES 4**

2 cups cashews

¼ cup Irish moss

½ cup plus 2 tablespoons filtered water

1 tablespoon fresh lemon juice

1 teaspoon apple cider vinegar

1¼ teaspoons Celtic sea salt

1¼ teaspoons coconut oil, plus more for greasing

One 12-oz. package mung bean pasta

EASY PRE-PREP:

1. Place the cashews in filtered water in a small bowl. Cover and refrigerate overnight.

2. Rinse the Irish moss very well in a colander until all of the sand is removed and the smell of the ocean is gone. Then place it in filtered water in a small bowl. Cover and refrigerate overnight.

1. Lightly oil a small rectangular loaf pan or mold with coconut oil.

2. Drain the cashews. Drain the Irish moss and place it in the pitcher of a Vitamix with ½ cup filtered water. Blend on high speed for 1 minute or until it is emulsified. Measure out 2 tablespoons and reserve the rest.

3. In a clean pitcher of the Vitamix, add the cashews, remaining 2 tablespoons water, emulsfied Irish moss, lemon juice, vinegar, salt, and coconut oil. Blend on medium speed, using the plunger to evenly distribute the mixture until smooth.

4. Transfer the mixture to the prepared loaf pan. Cover with parchment paper cut to fit the pan. Place the pan in the dehydrator and dehydrate at 90 degrees F for 24 hours. Refrigerate for 24 hours.

5. Boil the pasta according to the package directions. Drain and transfer to a serving bowl. Drop in 1-tablespoon dollops of cheese and toss to incorporate well. Garnish with fresh oregano and pine nuts.

N'EGGS BENNIE WITH HOLLANDAISE SAUCE AND COCONUT BACON

This new evolution of a creamy Hollandaise sauce will render you dreaming of Sunday brunch all week long. ■ **SERVES 1**

COCONUT BACON

1 teaspoon blue agave

1 tablespoon tamari

1 teaspoon liquid smoke

1 cup large coconut flakes

1 teaspoon smoked paprika

¼ teaspoon white pepper

N'EGGS BENNIE

One 12-ounce package silken tofu

⅛ teaspoon Indian black salt

2 bottom halves specialty bread from your favorite bakery

2 pieces romaine or butter lettuce

3 yellow cherry tomatoes

Celtic sea salt and freshly ground black pepper

Classic Hollandaise Sauce (page 45)

2 large basil leaves

FOR THE COCONUT BACON

1. Preheat the oven to 350 degrees F.

2. In a small bowl, combine all the ingredients and toss to coat.

3. Spread the mixture out onto a nonstick baking sheet and bake for 8 minutes, or until brown and crispy.

FOR THE N'EGGS BENNIE

1. Preheat the oven to 350 degrees F.

2. Drain the silken tofu and carefully remove it from the package. Place it on a cutting board or work surface.

3. Cut the tofu in a circular shape with a large fluted-edge cookie cutter or round 2-inch mold.

4. Slice each circular tofu shape crosswise so you have two identical pieces.

5. Using a spatula, carefully place both rounds on a rimmed baking sheet, sprinkle with black salt, which will provide the eggy, sulfur flavor, and bake for 10 minutes or until warm.

6. While the tofu is warming, arrange bread on a plate.

7. Top each half with a piece of romaine. Halve the tomatoes and set aside.

8. When the tofu is warm, remove it from the oven and carefully place each tofu round on top of the romaine, place tomato halves in the center of the tofu so make a "n'egg." Sprinkle with sea salt and pepper.

9. Smother the n'eggs in warm Hollandaise Sauce.

10. Sprinkle with Coconut Bacon and garnish with fresh basil.

DESSERTS

DEEP CLASSIC CHEESECAKE

CRÈME BRÛLÉE

MACLAY'S MEXICAN CHEESECAKE

BAKED ALMOND RICOTTA STRAWBERRY
SHORTCAKE

BANANA CREAM PIE

POACHED FIGS WITH MERINGUE

ALMOND COCONUT MACAROONS
WITH CRÈME FRAÎCHE

DEEP CLASSIC CHEESECAKE

A true divinity of flavor that will put a smile on every face at your table. ■ **SERVES 8**

CRUST

8 Medjool dates

1 teaspoon coconut oil

2 cups raw cashews

1 cup unsweetened dried shredded coconut

1 teaspoon Himalayan salt

FILLING

4 cups raw cashews

One 15-ounce can coconut milk

½ cup cocoa butter

1 cup premium light agave

1 vanilla bean, split lengthwise and the inside scraped out

1 teaspoon fresh lemon juice

3 pints fresh raspberries, for topping

EASY PRE-PREP:
Soak the dates in filtered water for at least 30 minutes. Drain and remove the pits.

FOR THE CRUST

1. Preheat the oven to 350 degrees F. Lightly oil the bottom and sides of a deep 6-inch springform pan with 1 teaspoon of coconut oil.

2. Roast the cashews on a rimmed baking sheet in the oven for 8 minutes.

3. In the bowl of a food processor, place the cashews and pulse six times or until the nuts are mealy in texture.

4. Add the shredded coconut and salt and pulse three times to incorporate well.

5. With the motor running, add the pitted dates one at a time and blend until the mixture balls up on the side of the bowl.

6. Transfer the crust mixture from the food processor to the prepared springform pan. Press the mixture down with your hands so that it covers the bottom of the pan evenly.

FOR THE FILLING

1. In the pitcher of a Vitamix, place the cashews, coconut milk, cocoa butter, agave, vanilla bean, and lemon juice. Blend on high speed for 2 minutes or until the mixture is smooth.

2. Pour the filling mixture into the prepared springform pan on top of the crust and place it in the freezer overnight.

3. Thaw for 30 minutes before serving. Remove the springform sides and decorate with the fresh raspberries. Begin in the center and place them in a circular pattern, spiraling out until the entire top is covered. Serve.

CRÈME BRÛLÉE

This dessert is so rich, full bodied, and creamy that it will leave you doubting it's dairy-free. Invest in a chef's torch and you'll be able to create that perfect caramelized top. ■ **MAKES THREE 2-INCH RAMEKINS**

2 cups cashews

⅔ cup hardened coconut milk (from a 15-ounce can of organic coconut milk)

¼ cup cocoa butter

½ cup aquafaba (liquid from canned garbanzo beans)

3 tablespoons light agave syrup

1 teaspoon vanilla extract

½ cup organic sugar

EASY PRE-PREP:

1. Place the cashews in filtered water in a small bowl. Cover and refrigerate overnight.

2. Place the can of coconut milk in the fridge overnight.

---

1. Open the can of coconut milk and scoop out the hardened coconut milk, discarding the liquid.

2. Drain the cashews. In the pitcher of a Vitamix, place the hardened coconut milk, cashews, cocoa butter, aquafaba, agave, and vanilla. Blend on medium speed, using the plunger to evenly distribute the mixture until very smooth. Then, process on high speed for 1 more minute until silky smooth.

3. Divide the filling evenly among the three ramekins, cover with parchment rounds cut to fit the ramekins, and chill for at least 2 hours. Remove from the fridge and sprinkle the sugar on the top.

4. Use a chef's torch to torch the sugar until it is golden brown and hardened. Follow torch manufacturer's directions.

5. Crack open the top with your spoon and devour!

MACLAY'S MEXICAN CHEESECAKE

Raw, decadent, and bursting with contrasting flavors, this antioxidant creation of delish takes cheesecake to a whole new level. ■ **SERVES 8**

4 cups raw cashews

10 Medjool dates

1 teaspoon coconut oil, for greasing the pan

3 cups raw walnuts

½ teaspoon Himalayan salt

¼ teaspoon cayenne pepper, plus more for dusting

One 15-ounce can coconut milk

1 cup premium light agave

5 tablespoons raw cacao powder

1 teaspoon cinnamon, plus more for dusting

¼ cup cacao nibs for garnish

EASY PRE-PREP:
Place the cashews in filtered water in a medium bowl. Cover and refrigerate overnight. Place the dates in water in a small bowl. Cover and refrigerate overnight.

1. Lightly oil a 13-inch springform pan with coconut oil.

2. In the bowl of a food processor, place the walnuts and pulse until mealy.

3. Drain the water from the dates, and remove and discard the pits.

4. With the motor running, add the dates to the bowl of the food processor one at a time and blend until the dough balls up on the side of the bowl.

5. Press the dough into the bottom of the prepared springform pan in an even layer. Sprinkle with salt and cayenne.

6. In the pitcher of a Vitamix, place the cashews, coconut milk, agave, cacao powder, and cinnamon. Blend on medium speed for 30 seconds, then increase to high speed and blend for 1 minute more or until the filling is smooth.

7. Pour the filling into the crust and smooth out with a rubber spatula.

8. Freeze the pie in for at least 8 hours or overnight. Remove and let stand 30 minutes before serving. Garnish with cacao nibs and cinnamon.

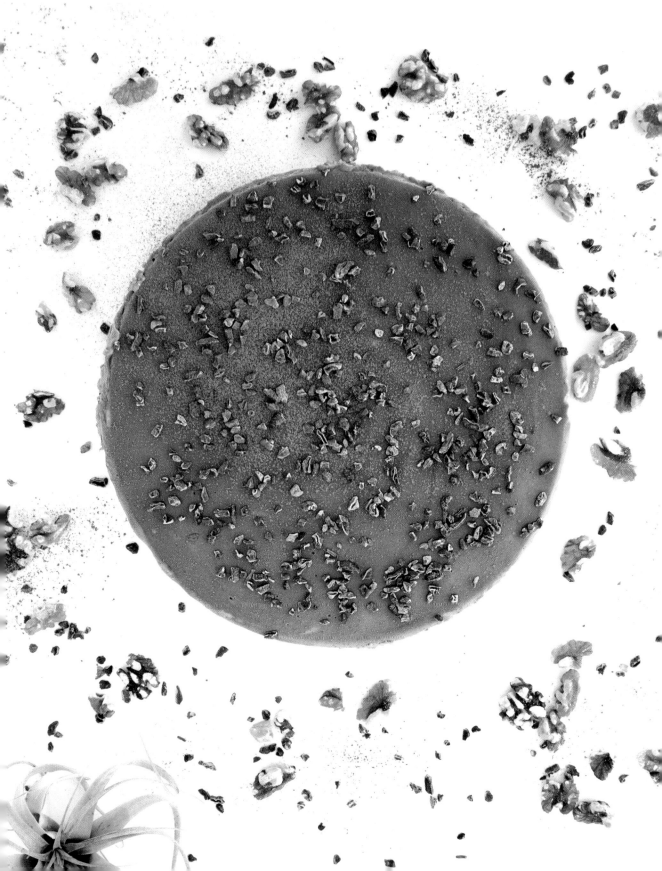

BAKED ALMOND RICOTTA STRAWBERRY SHORTCAKE

Baking nut cheese creates
a cake-like savory treat.

■ SERVES 6

**One 4-inch round Sprouted Almond
Coconut Ricotta (page 112)**

2 tablespoons coconut oil

**1 pint fresh organic strawberries,
sliced**

¼ cup organic sugar

1. Preheat the oven to 400 degrees F.

2. Bake the Sprouted Almond Coconut
   Ricotta cheese inside its mold for
   10 minutes or until the top develops a
   crust. Brush the top with coconut oil and
   continue baking for 40 minutes or until
   golden brown. Remove from the oven.
   Remove the baked cheese from the mold
   and transfer to a plate.

3. Slice the strawberries crosswise. Stack
   the strawberries on top of the cheese and
   sprinkle with the sugar.

BANANA CREAM PIE

Roasting the coconut and nuts for this crust brings a warm flavor that is a beautiful contrast to the creamy cool texture of the filling. I love to serve this in a shallow hand-painted ceramic dish so that you see the pattern as you remove slices. ■ **MAKES ONE 9-INCH PIE**

FILLING

Two 15-ounce cans coconut milk

3 ripe bananas (not overripe)

1 teaspoon lemon juice

½ cup cocoa butter

CRUST

8 Medjool dates

1 teaspoon coconut oil, for greasing the pie dish

1 cup shredded dried coconut

½ cup macadamia nuts

¾ cup pine nuts

1 teaspoon large-grain Celtic sea salt

CREAM TOPPING

¼ cup aquafaba (liquid from canned garbanzo beans)

¼ cup organic powdered sugar

1 firm banana, sliced, for garnish

2 tablespoons coconut flakes, for garnish

EASY PRE-PREP:
Place the cans of coconut milk in the refrigerator overnight.

FOR THE CRUST

1. Soak the dates in filtered water for at least 30 minutes. Drain, and discard the pits (you can compost them). Set the dates aside.

2. Preheat the oven to 350 degrees F. Lightly oil a 9-inch ceramic pie dish with the coconut oil.

3. On a rimmed baking sheet, arrange the coconut in a thin layer and toast for about 5 minutes or until golden.

4. On another rimmed baking sheet, arrange the macadamia nuts and pine nuts separately on the pan and roast for 8 to 10 minutes, until golden brown.

5. In the bowl of a food processor, pulse the macadamia nuts until mealy.

6. Add the pine nuts and pulse again to incorporate well.

7. Add the coconut and pulse a few more times.

8. With the motor running, add the dates one at a time until the mixture balls up on one side of the bowl.

(recipe continues)

9. Press the crust into the bottom of the pie dish evenly.

10. Sprinkle the salt over the crust.

FOR THE FILLING

1. Scoop out the hardened part of the coconut milk from the cans, discarding the liquid, and place the coconut milk in the pitcher of a Vitamix or high-powered blender. Add the bananas, lemon juice, and cocoa butter and process on high speed for 2 minutes.

2. Pour the filling into the crust and smooth out with a spatula.

FOR THE CREAM TOPPING

1. In the bowl of a stand mixer, place the aquafaba. Whip at high speed for 5 minutes.

2. Add the powdered sugar and continue to whip until stiff peaks form, approximately 15 minutes.

3. Spread over the custard. Top with the banana slices and coconut flakes.

4. Slice and serve!

POACHED FIGS WITH MERINGUE

A natural beauty! Who knew that aquafaba could produce stiff peaks that hold their own next to any egg white? Now you do! ■ **SERVES 6**

¼ cup aquafaba (liquid from canned garbanzo beans)

1 cup organic powdered sugar

1 cup organic coconut sugar

1 cup red wine

8 fresh figs, halved

1 teaspoon lemon zest

Fresh mint, for garnish

1. In the bowl of a stand mixer, place the aquafaba and powdered sugar. Whip at high speed for 10 to 15 minutes to form silky peaks. Transfer the meringue in the metal bowl to the refrigerator to chill.

2. In a small saucepan over medium heat, place the coconut sugar and red wine. Stir to dissolve the coconut sugar and bring the mixture to a gentle boil, until it thickens. Add the figs, turning to coat.

3. On a serving platter, arrange the figs. Spoon the meringue over the top. Garnish with lemon zest and fresh mint.

ALMOND COCONUT MACAROONS WITH CRÈME FRAÎCHE

Who doesn't love the fresh, chewy taste of this delicious cookie? This version is *magnifique* with a dollop of crème fraîche. ■ **MAKES 12 MACAROONS**

1 tablespoon coconut oil, plus more for greasing the baking sheet

4 cups shredded dried coconut

2 tablespoons aquafaba (liquid from canned garbanzo beans)

1 tablespoon light agave

1 tablespoon maple syrup

1 teaspoon almond extract

Crème Fraîche (page 184)

1. Preheat the oven to 375 degrees F. Cover a baking sheet with parchment paper or grease the baking sheet with coconut oil.

2. In the bowl of a food processor, place the coconut, aquafaba, agave, maple syrup, and almond extract. Process for 1 minute until a doughlike mixture forms.

3. Using a small melon scooper, arrange the macaroons about 1 inch apart on the prepared baking sheet.

4. Bake for 8 minutes or until browned. Transfer to a serving plate and top with dollops of crème fraîche.

NUT-FREE CHEESES & SPREADS

QUICK CHICKPEA CHEESY SPREAD

MALIBU MOMMA'S SUNFLOWER SEED CHEESE

JUNE'S CREAMY SESAME SEED SPREAD

WHITE BEAN CHEESE

FAUX-QUEFORT

FETA TOFU CHEESE

QUICK CHICKPEA CHEESY SPREAD

Wondering what to do with those leftover garbanzo beans from all that aquafaba? I dreamed up this tasty cheese as one delicious solution. Garbanzo beans require the healthy fat of coconut oil to give it the texture and consistency of fresh cheese. ■ **MAKES 2 CUPS**

¼ cup Irish moss

½ cup filtered water

2 tablespoons refined coconut oil, plus more for greasing the cheese mold

2 cups canned garbanzo beans or one 15.5-ounce can of garbanzo beans, drained (reserve the aquafaba for other recipes)

1 teaspoon garlic powder

1 teaspoon Celtic sea salt

2 tablespoons chickpea miso paste

1 teaspoon fresh lemon juice

¼ cup nutritional yeast

EASY PRE-PREP:
Rinse the Irish moss very well in a colander until all the sand is removed and the smell of the ocean is gone. Then place it in filtered water in a small bowl. Cover and refrigerate overnight.

1. Lightly oil a 4-inch cheese mold with coconut oil.

2. Drain the Irish moss and place it in the bowl of a Vitamix with the water. Blend on high speed for 1 minute or until it is emulsified. Measure out 2 tablespoons and reserve the rest.

3. In a clean bowl of the Vitamix, place the emulsified Irish moss, garbanzo beans, garlic powder, salt, miso, lemon juice, and nutritional yeast.

4. Blend on medium-high speed, using the plunger to evenly distribute the mixture until smooth.

5. Pour the mixture into the prepared cheese mold and refrigerate for 8 hours or overnight.

6. Turn the cheese out of the mold onto a serving platter. Using a butter knife, shape the cheese and smooth out the texture or transfer into a serving bowl.

MALIBU MOMMA'S SUNFLOWER SEED CHEESE

A divine nut-free alternative that doesn't sacrifice taste or texture! ■ **MAKES 2 CUPS**

2 cups sunflower seeds

1 large garlic clove

1 teaspoon fresh lemon juice

1 teaspoon Celtic sea salt

1 teaspoon refined coconut oil

1 teaspoon fresh chives, for garnish

EASY PRE-PREP:
Soak the sunflower seeds in filtered water in a small bowl for 4 hours, then drain and rinse multiple times throughout the day for 24 hours to sprout. They can be left on the counter covered with a piece of cheesecloth. Use immediately.

1. In the pitcher of a Vitamix, place the sunflower seeds, garlic, lemon juice, salt, and coconut oil. Blend on medium speed, using the plunger to evenly distribute the mixture until smooth.

2. Take a layer of fine cheesecloth and stretch it over the mouth of a small bowl. Turn the bowl upside down to tie it off and secure it. Once the cheesecloth is secured, turn the bowl upright.

3. Transfer the cheese to the cheesecloth, cover with more cheesecloth, and place the bowl in the refrigerator. Let the cheese drain for 24 hours.

4. Transfer the cheese to a serving dish and sprinkle chives on top.

JUNE'S CREAMY SESAME SEED SPREAD

An easy, tasty spread that works amazingly with appetizers or as a side to your steamed veggies. ■ **MAKES 2 CUPS**

2 cups light sesame seeds

5 tablespoons fresh lemon juice

2 teaspoons Celtic sea salt

2 tablespoons refined coconut oil

½ teaspoon light agave

Seaweed, for garnish

EASY PRE-PREP:
Place the sesame seeds in water in a small bowl. Add 1 tablespoon of the lemon juice and soak overnight, covered, in the refrigerator. The following day, drain the sesame seeds into a fine sieve.

1. In the pitcher of a Vitamix, place the sesame seeds, remaining 4 tablespoons of lemon juice, salt, coconut oil, and agave. Blend on medium speed, using the plunger to distribute the mixture well.

2. Transfer to a decorative shell or serving dish. Garnish with seaweed.

WHITE BEAN CHEESE

White beans make a mouthwatering delicious nut-free base for any cheese. The best part is there is no need for aging the cheese. When using beans as a cheese base, you need to add more coconut oil so that it has enough healthy fat to set up. This is a great allergy-free recipe to have in the rotation even if you aren't allergic to nuts. ■ **MAKES 2 CUPS**

¼ cup Irish moss

½ cup filtered water

3 tablespoons unrefined coconut oil, plus more for greasing the cheese mold

2 cups canned white or great Northern beans, drained from their liquid

1 teaspoon garlic powder

1 teaspoon Himalayan salt

2 tablespoons chickpea miso paste

1 teaspoon fresh lemon juice

2 tablespoons nutritional yeast

Crackers or nuts, for garnish

EASY PRE-PREP:
Rinse the Irish moss very well in a colander until all the sand is removed and the smell the ocean is gone. Then place it in filtered water in a small bowl. Cover and refrigerate overnight.

1. Lightly oil a 4-inch cheese mold.

2. Drain the Irish moss and place it in the pitcher of a Vitamix with the water. Blend on high for 1 minute or until it is emulsified. Measure out 2 tablespoons and reserve the rest.

3. In a clean pitcher of the Vitamix, place the emulsified Irish moss, the beans, garlic powder, salt, miso, lemon juice, coconut oil, and nutritional yeast. Blend on medium speed, using the plunger to evenly distribute the mixture until well incorporated and smooth. You may have to scrape down the sides a few times using a rubber spatula.

4. Transfer the cheese to the prepared cheese mold.

5. Cover with a parchment round and refrigerate overnight. To serve, turn the cheese onto a serving platter. Using your hands and a smooth knife, shape and smooth out the cheese. Crush crackers or nuts and press them into the sides.

FAUX-QUEFORT

An allergen-free creative spin on roquefort. I use more salt and flavorings here because of the tofu in this recipe. The cheese soaks up the salty taste while it's setting up in the fridge. Feel free to experiment with increasing the amount of nutritional yeast. ■ **MAKES 1½ CUPS OR ONE 6X3-INCH DEEP TART PAN**

2 tablespoons coconut oil, plus more for greasing the pan

¼ cup Irish moss

½ cup filtered water

½ cup fresh coconut meat from a brown coconut (do not substitute with coconut flakes)

1 cup organic sprouted tofu, plus ¼ cup for the crumble

¼ cup aquafaba (liquid from canned garbanzo beans)

3 teaspoons apple cider vinegar

2 teaspoons plus ½ teaspoon Celtic sea salt

2 tablespoons nutritional yeast

Freshly cracked black pepper

½ teaspoon powdered spirulina

EASY PRE-PREP:
Rinse the Irish moss very well in a colander until all the sand is removed and the smell of the ocean is gone. Then, place it in filtered water in a small bowl. Cover and refrigerate overnight.

1. Oil a 6-inch springform pan with coconut oil.

2. Drain the Irish moss and place it in the pitcher of a Vitamix with the water. Blend on high speed for 1 minute or until it is emulsified. Measure out 2 tablespoons and set aside.

3. In the bowl of a food processor, place the coconut meat and pulse until mealy in texture. Set aside.

4. Drain the tofu and measure out three-quarters of the package (reserve the remaining for a tofu scramble). Press out the excess water using paper towels. Apply strong pressure and remove as much water as possible.

5. In the pitcher of a Vitamix, place the emulsified Irish moss, coconut meat, tofu, aquafaba, coconut oil, vinegar, and 2 teaspoons salt.

6. Blend on medium speed, using the plunger to evenly distribute the mixture until well incorporated.

7. Pour the mixture into the prepared pan.

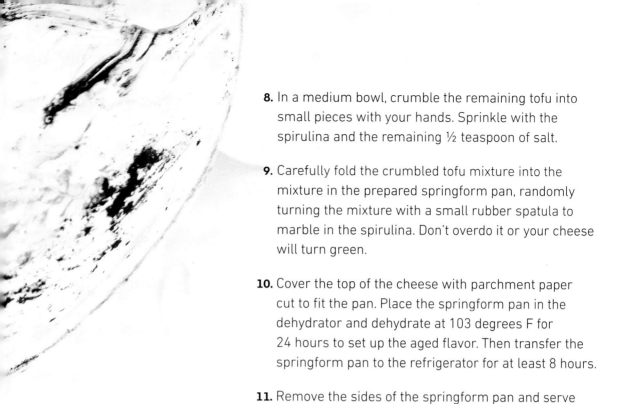

8. In a medium bowl, crumble the remaining tofu into small pieces with your hands. Sprinkle with the spirulina and the remaining ½ teaspoon of salt.

9. Carefully fold the crumbled tofu mixture into the mixture in the prepared springform pan, randomly turning the mixture with a small rubber spatula to marble in the spirulina. Don't overdo it or your cheese will turn green.

10. Cover the top of the cheese with parchment paper cut to fit the pan. Place the springform pan in the dehydrator and dehydrate at 103 degrees F for 24 hours to set up the aged flavor. Then transfer the springform pan to the refrigerator for at least 8 hours.

11. Remove the sides of the springform pan and serve the cheese with crackers.

FETA TOFU CHEESE

Allergy-free and full of flavor. This recipe makes a masterpiece of ordinary tofu.

■ MAKES 1 CUP

1 cup organic sprouted tofu

2 tablespoons refined coconut oil

1 teaspoon lactic acid (made from sugar beets)

3 teaspoons apple cider vinegar

½ teaspoon Celtic sea salt

1 teaspoon Himalayan salt

½ teaspoon garlic powder

1 teaspoon fresh lemon juice

2 teaspoons Greek spices or za'atar (a blend of thyme, oregano, and marjoram)

1. Press the tofu between layers of paper towels, using the heels of your hands to release the moisture.

2. In the bowl of a food processor, crumble the pressed tofu and add the coconut oil, lactic acid, vinegar, salts, garlic powder, lemon juice, and spices.

3. Process on medium speed until the mixture is well incorporated.

4. Transfer the cheese to a shallow serving dish and smooth out the top with a rubber spatula.

5. Cover and refrigerate overnight. Use in Greek Salad Stack (page 128).

VARIATION:

1. After pressing the water from the tofu, cut it into small ½-inch cubes.

2. Place all of the seasonings in the bottom of a medium bowl (subbing olive oil for coconut oil), mix in the tofu cubes, and toss to coat.

3. Transfer the cubes to a mason jar and cover.

4. Refrigerate for 48 hours before serving.

DAIRY-FREE STAPLES

CRÈME FRAÎCHE

CLASSIC SOUR CREAM

YOGURT, 2 WAYS
  Tangy Coconut Yogurt with Blackstrap
  Molasses
  Easy Overnight Yogurt

KALE CHIP CRACKERS

BUCKWHEAT CRACKERS

BERRY CRACKERS

CRÈME FRAÎCHE

The rich, velvety texture pairs perfectly with my Almond Coconut Macaroons (page 167). ■ **MAKES 2 CUPS**

2 cups cashews

½ teaspoon refined coconut oil, for greasing the pans

¾ cup aquafaba (liquid from canned garbanzo beans)

½ teaspoon lemon juice

EASY PRE-PREP:
Place the cashews in filtered water in a small bowl. Cover and refrigerate overnight.

1. Lightly oil two 4-inch springform pans with coconut oil.

2. Drain the cashews. In the pitcher of a Vitamix, place the cashews, aquafaba, and lemon juice.

3. Blend on medium speed, using the plunger to evenly distribute the mixture until well incorporated. Transfer the crème fraîche into the prepared springform pans, smoothing the top with a rubber spatula.

4. Cover with a round of parchment paper. Place the springform pans in the dehydrator and dehydrate at 90 degrees F overnight.

5. Using an ice cream scooper, remove the crème fraîche and transfer it to a glass storage container. It will keep stored for about 1 week.

CLASSIC SOUR CREAM

The rich, creamy condiment goes beautifully with my fluffy Stuffed Red Potato Bites (page 124). ■ MAKES 2 CUPS

2 cups cashews

½ teaspoon refined coconut oil, for greasing the pans

¾ cup aquafaba (liquid from canned garbanzo beans)

3 teaspoons apple cider vinegar or 1 cap acidophilus (3-billion-active-culture strain)

EASY PRE-PREP:
Place the cashews in filtered water in a small bowl. Cover and refrigerate overnight.

1. Lightly oil two 4-inch springform pans with coconut oil.

2. Drain the cashews. In the pitcher of a Vitamix, place the cashews, aquafaba, and apple cider vinegar. Blend on medium speed, using the plunger to evenly distribute the mixture until well incorporated.

3. Transfer into mason jars filling them only half full to leave room for the sour cream to expand. Cover with a lid.

4. Dehydrate in the dehydrator at 108 degrees F overnight.

5. Open the mason jars and stir the sour cream until smooth. This will keep stored for about 1 week.

YOGURT, 2 WAYS

TANGY COCONUT YOGURT WITH BLACKSTRAP MOLASSES

Smooth and silky doesn't even begin to describe the symphony of textures in this recipe. The health benefits of blackstrap molasses are so impressive, we would benefit greatly by eating it outside of holiday gingerbread cookies! ■ **MAKES 2 CUPS**

Meat from 1 young coconut (the variety you drink coconut water from), plus ½ cup coconut water

1 capsule acidophilus (3-billion-active-culture strain)

1 teaspoon coconut oil

4 medjool dates, pitted and quartered

1 teaspoon blackstrap molasses

1 teaspoon hemp seeds, for garnish

EASY PRE-PREP:
Using a coco-jack, open the coconut, reserve the water, and scoop out the meat.

1. In the pitcher of a Vitamix, place the coconut meat, coconut water, acidophilus, and coconut oil.

2. Blend on high speed until smooth.

3. Fill two mason jars half full, leaving room for the yogurt to rise. Screw on the lids, place the jars in the dehydrator, and dehydrate at 108 degrees F overnight.

4. In the morning remove the lids and stir the yogurt until smooth.

5. To serve: In a short glass, place the dates in a layer on the bottom. Spoon one jar of yogurt on top, and drizzle the blackstrap molasses over the yogurt. Garnish with hemp seeds.

EASY OVERNIGHT YOGURT

A coconut nut-based yogurt that is thick, tangy, and velvety. Get creative by infusing it with your favorite flavors and toppings! ■ **SERVES 2**

½ cup coconut meat from a young green coconut (the variety you drink coconut water from)

¼ cup raw cashews

6 tablespoons filtered water

½ capsule acidophilus (3-billion-active-culture strain)

EASY PRE-PREP:
Place the cashews in filtered water in a small bowl. Cover and refrigerate overnight.

1. Drain the cashews. In the pitcher of a Vitamix, place the coconut, cashews, water, and acidophilus. Blend on high speed for 2 minutes or until smooth.

2. Transfer into mason jars filling them only half full to leave room for the yogurt to expand. Cover with a lid.

3. Dehydrate in the dehydrator at 108 degrees F overnight.

4. Open the mason jars and stir the yogurt until smooth. Add sweetener or fruit.

5. Serve over granola.

KALE CHIP CRACKERS

Kale crackers are deliciously healthy and add a gorgeous boost of color to your superfood cracker box. ■ MAKES TWENTY 2-INCH CRACKERS

1 cup flaxseeds, preferably yellow, ground in a blender

4 cups curly kale, stems removed

⅔ cup nutritional yeast

2 teaspoons Celtic sea salt

1 teaspoon garlic powder

1 teaspoon cumin

1 cup filtered water

1. In the pitcher of a Vitamix or high-speed blender, place the flaxseeds, kale, nutritional yeast, salt, garlic powder, cumin, and water. Blend on medium speed until the mixture liquefies.

2. Spread the mixture thinly and evenly on a Teflex sheet (the sheet that comes with the dehydrator).

3. Score to the desired cracker shape.

4. Place the Teflex sheet in the dehydrator and dehydrate the crackers on high for 2 hours, then dehydrate at 135 degrees F for 2 additional hours.

BUCKWHEAT CRACKERS

Once you get the hang of making crackers in your dehydrator, your creative juices will start to flow. These tasty creations are fundamental to mastering the raw cracker. ■ **MAKES SIXTEEN 2-INCH CRACKERS**

2 cups buckwheat

1 cup chopped red bell pepper

1 cup carrot pulp (enjoy the juice while you prep)

⅓ cup fresh basil or cilantro

1 teaspoon Celtic sea salt

⅛ teaspoon cayenne pepper

2 tablespoons tamari

2 teaspoons maple syrup

2 teaspoons garlic powder

EASY PRE-PREP:

Soak the buckwheat in a medium bowl overnight.

1. In the pitcher of a Vitamix place the buckwheat, bell peppers, carrot pulp, herbs, salt, cayenne, tamari, maple syrup, and garlic powder. Blend on medium speed until smooth.

2. Spread the mixture thinly and evenly onto a Teflex sheet (the sheet that comes with the dehydrator).

3. Place the Teflex sheet in the dehydrator and dehydrate the sheet of crackers at 145 degrees F for 4 hours.

4. Score your cracker sizes and return them to the dehydrator reducing the temp to 105 degrees F for another 6 hours or until dry.

5. Remove the crackers from the sheet. The crackers should break off easily along the slice marks.

6. Store in a glass cookie jar or in sealed plastic bags.

BERRY CRACKERS

A sweeter cracker with a mix of textures that complement cheddars, goudas, and provolones alike. ■ **MAKES SIXTEEN 2-INCH CRACKERS**

1 cup raspberries

1 cup blackberries

1 cup buckwheat

½ cup walnuts

1 cup almond meal

½ cup maple syrup

EASY PRE-PREP:
Soak the buckwheat in filtered water in a medium bowl overnight.

1. In the bowl of a food processor, place the raspberries, blackberries, buckwheat, walnuts, almond meal, and maple syrup. Process for 2 minutes or until smooth.

2. Smooth out the dough into a thin layer (as thin as possible) on a Teflex sheet (the sheet that comes with the dehydrator). Then cover the dough with a second dehydrator sheet and roll it with a rolling pin.

3. Place the Teflex sheet in the dehydrator and dehydrate the sheet of dough at 145 degrees F for 3 hours.

4. Peel the dough off the Teflex sheet and move it onto a plastic mesh sheet. Dehydrate for 8 hours more or until firm and dry.

5. Remove the crackers from the sheet. The crackers should break off easily along the slice marks.

6. Store in a glass cookie jar or in sealed plastic bags.

ACKNOWLEDGMENTS & RESOURCES

All love to my beloved food photographer and assistant Leia Vita Marasovich, I share this book with you. Your photographs are gorgeous! Thank you for your conscious eyes, expanded perspective, and pure loving heart in each moment of this journey. I am blessed to share so many precious moments with you. I hope our collaborations never end.

Deep gratitude to Megan Newman, Lucia Watson, Anne Kosmoski, Ashley Tucker, Farin Schlussel, Nina Caldas, and the entire team at Avery/Penguin Random House for their unwavering support and beautiful design of this book. It was a powerful expansive women's collaboration that elevated the book beyond what any of us could have done alone. I adore working with you beauties.

Namaste to Byrd Leavell, my agent. To share the name "Byrd" (my childhood nickname) with someone so rare is a significant sign from the Universe. Thanks for holding space for me to draw my cosmic threads into physical expressions.

Gene Baur, Lindsay, and the crew at Farm Sanctuary, who allowed me to come in and be photographed with their cows (www.farmsanctuary.org).

Bruno, William, and Edward, three of the rescue dairy cows at Farm Sanctuary, for receiving me with gentle kindness and allowing me to wrap my arms around you and smother you with kisses.

Jules Tolentino, the coolest bass player around, who also served as my sous chef in the early stages of this book. Cook with me again when your tour ends?

Maggie Curtis, my niece, sous chef, and organizational wizard with the best handwriting on the planet. When you are around, everything flows easier. Thank you for supporting me.

Juana Alvarenga, who prepped my kitchen space, making it shiny and clean—not my strong suit. A clean kitchen allows me to create prolifically. Thank you for all the love and care you gave me.

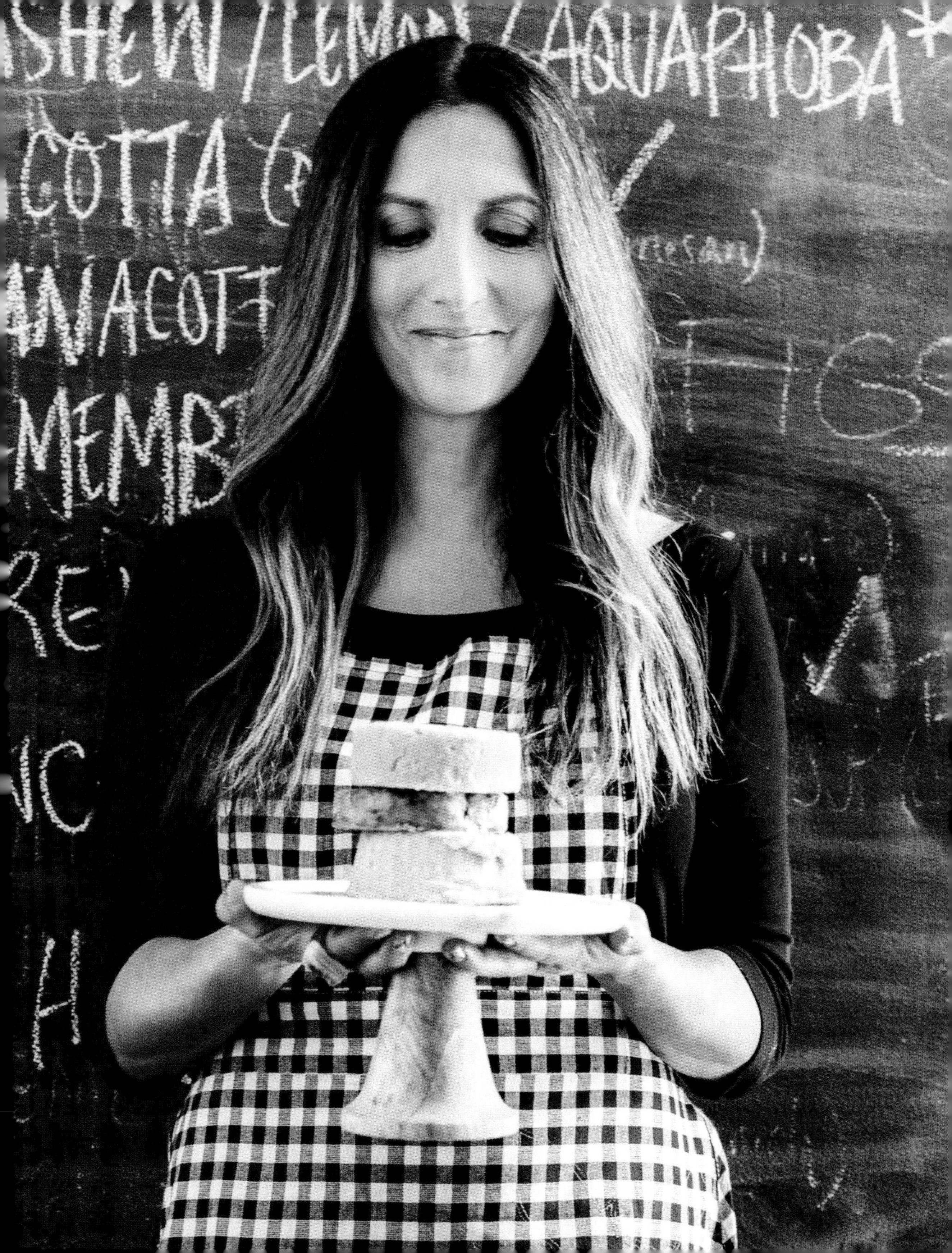
AQUAPHOBA*

Maclay Heriot, photographer of *The Plantpower Way*. Thank you for your amazing photographs of me with the Farm Sanctuary Cows. You captured a divine experience with such heart.

Daniel Johnson, photographer for my brand images and also for my author photos. Thank you for your beautiful eye and for seeing me.

Shyama Grace and Jennie Halpern, makeup and hair, for making me look good.

Conscious filmmakers Daryl Wien and Zoe Lister Jones; Daryl came up with the best title ever for this book! It has been a blessing to know you both and to share so many precious moments in the world of wellness and also on this journey of transformation. Resist, or even better, Insist!

June Louks, my dear friend and author of *Malibu Mom's Manifesto*, master gardener, and spiritual sister committed to healing this planet. Thank you for sharing your crackers and nut-free cheese for this book, and for your limitless love.

My testers and tasters: Paula Murphy; Rob Bell; Plantpower Way Tribe; Lucy Pinter and Jan Welters; and Tamara, Mathew, and Grayson Wilder.

Ta Ma Ra, for her spiritual blessings and guidance, and April, for her spiritual wisdom.

Roxy Faye Made, for gifting us gorgeous handmade ceramics on which to shoot my cheese.

Shawn Patterson, for your beautiful layouts in the early stages, which led to this book coming to fruition.

I tasted my first nut cheese in the dining room of Real Food Daily in Santa Monica over ten years ago. Ann Gentry, the founder, has been a force for eating consciously for a very long time.

Mathew and Terces of Cafe Gratitude, who created fresher, gentler cheese using coconut meat and Irish moss, and opened a world of new possibilities for all of us.

Mathew Kenny, founder of Plant Food and Wine Culinary school, who gifted me a weekend cheese and chocolate workshop with educator Casey Dozel.

Miyoko, author and pioneer of plant-based cheese. Miyoko has her own line of in-store cheese. She paved the road for this book to be possible.

I thank Greg, Yvonne, Julian, and Kyra Anzalone, for believing in Rich and in me and for providing the support to realize our dreams and missions.

My gorgeous Mother, Vylna "Abuela" Rosado Mathis, for knowing that I was on to something big.

My beautiful tribe, Hari, Tyler, Trapper, Mathis, and Jaya for always believing in me . . .

Rich Roll, for your love and devotion to our marriage and for sharing this incredible journey with me, which has touched so many. I love you eternally.

OTHER BOOKS AND PROJECTS BY JULIE PIATT (AKA SRIMATI)

The Plantpower Way: Whole Food Plant-Based Recipes and Guidance for the Whole Family, Rich Roll and Julie Piatt

Plantpower Italia (coming 2018)

Online video courses with mindbodygreen: "The Ultimate Guide to Plant-Based Nutrition," Rich Roll and Julie Piatt; " How to Build a Conscious Relationship and Experience the Deepest Intimacy of Your Life," Julie Piatt and Rich Roll

BOOKS

The Non-Dairy Evolution Cookbook by Skye Michael Conroy, who presents a comprehensive body of recipes and techniques in this invaluable book.

A Malibu Mom's Manifesto on Whole Foods by June Louks, which contains nut-free cheeses and processes that she created along with her family over many years of growing her own food and eating for health.

The Cheese Trap by Dr. Neal Barnard reveals the shocking truth about cheese—the dangerous addiction that is harming your health—and presents a radical program to lose weight and feel great.

FILMS

Consumed by filmmakers Daryl Wein and Zoe Lister Jones is the first major narrative feature film to tackle head-on the complex world of genetically modified foods and its negative impact on our food, farmers, and children.

Cowspiracy: The Sustainability Secret is a groundbreaking feature-length environmental documentary following intrepid filmmaker Kip Andersen as he uncovers the most destructive industry facing the planet today—animal agriculture—and investigates why the world's leading environmental organizations are too afraid to talk about it. By Kip Andersen and Keegan Kuhn.

What the Health uncovers the secret to preventing and even reversing chronic diseases—and investigates why the nation's leading health organizations don't want us to know about it. Also by filmmakers Kip Anderson and Keegan Kuhn.

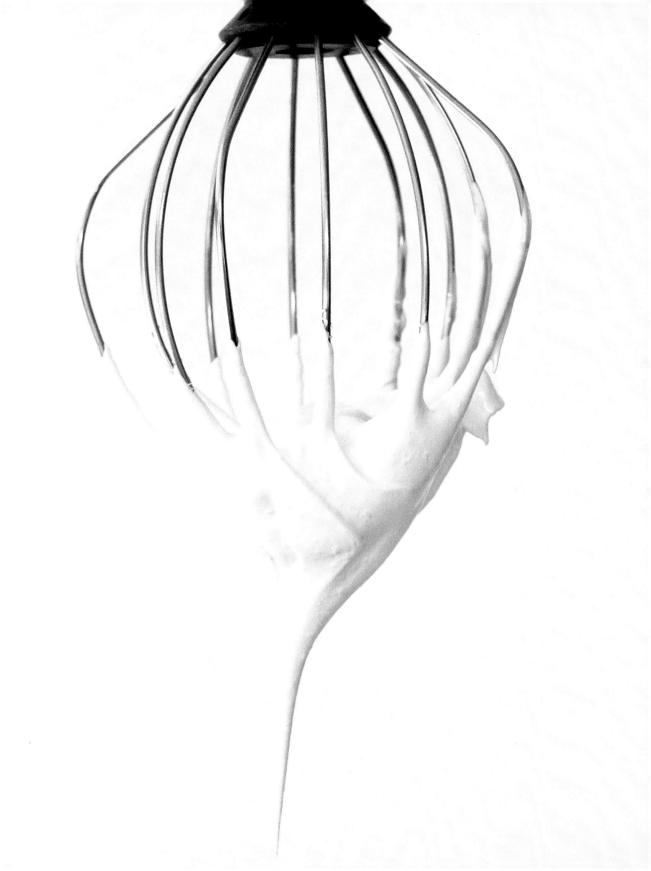

INDEX

Page numbers in *italics* refer to photos.

...EESE	PESTO	CREAM CHEES...
...RGONZOLA	OLIVE CILANTRO	SOUR CREAM
...E CREAM	SMOKED CHEDDAR	TRUFFLE CASH...
...IE	~~SUNFLOWER SEED~~	GOAT CHEESE...
...EMBERT	~~TOFU FETA HERBED~~	GOAT CHEESE (...
...OUDA	AGED TOFU	CREME FRAICH...
...OVALONE	o McCLAY'S CHEESECAKE	YOGURT (tart...
...EDDAR	o MACLAY'S ENCH. SAUCE	MARSCAPONE
...ZARELLA	+ EGGS BENEDICT	BURRATA
...TA	+ GRANOLA	CHILI PEPPER
...MESAN //AGED, HARD *	+ PIE (whipped cream)	CUMIN AZTEC
...MESAN/CRUMBLED *	+ ABALONE MUSHR. (parmesan)	MISO JAPANE...
...IPPED CREAM	~~+ GREEK SALAD (feta)~~	PINE NUT OLIV...
...REAM CHEESE (flavor 2)	+ HEIRLOOM BASIL SALAD (burrata)	APPLE SPINA...
...REAM CHEESE (flavor 3)	+ PIZZA (mozarella)	CHICKORY ROA...
...YOGURT (flavor 2)	+ GRILLED CHEESE/TOMATO SOUP (cheddar)	GORGONZOL...
...YOGURT (flavor 3)	+ FRUIT (camembert)	LINGUINI KA...
...PEPPER JACK	+ FRUIT (brie)	BEET RAVI...
	+ CREME BRULEÉ (creme fraich)	RICOTTA (one...
FONDUE	+ AU GRATIN (marscapone)	+ AVOCADO TO...
~~ETTUCINE (alfredo)~~	+ LASAGNA (ricotta)	+ BAKED POTA...
...OLLANDAISE	+ POACHED APPLES (bleu cheese)	+ BEET SALAD
...AC N' CHEESE	+ PASTA (bleu cheese)	PREP
...SIL, SUNDRIED TOMATO	+ PANINI (provalone)	RICOTTA (fr...
...LIVE ROSMARY	GARBANZO MISO *	
...EMON DILL PEPPERCORN	BLEU CHEESE *	
...NACHO SAUCE	GARBANZO/LEMON JUICE	
...ARM QUESO FRESCO	CASHEW/LEMON J./AQUAPHOBA	
	CASHEW / ½ ACIDOPHILUS	

ALSO BY JULIE PIATT

WITH RICH ROLL

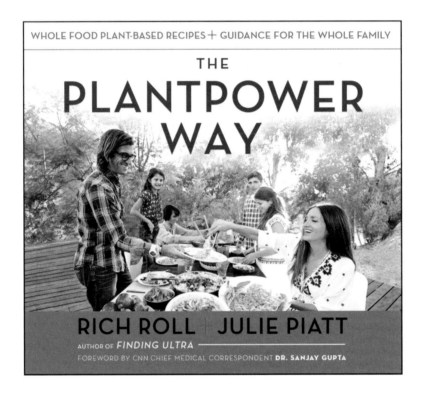

WHOLE FOOD PLANT-BASED RECIPES + GUIDANCE FOR THE WHOLE FAMILY

THE

PLANTPOWER WAY

RICH ROLL | **JULIE PIATT**

AUTHOR OF *FINDING ULTRA*

FOREWORD BY CNN CHIEF MEDICAL CORRESPONDENT **DR. SANJAY GUPTA**

A TRANSFORMATIVE FAMILY LIFESTYLE GUIDE ON THE POWER OF PLANT-BASED EATING—WITH 120 RECIPES.

SRIMATI.COM

HROLL.COM

AVERY